The Captain

of the

Juniper

Wayne E. Beyea

iUniverse, Inc.
New York   Bloomington

The Captain of the Juniper

Copyright © 2008 by Wayne E. Beyea

iUniverse books may be ordered through booksellers or by contacting:

iUniverse
1663 Liberty Drive
Bloomington, IN 47403
www.iuniverse.com
1-800-Authors (1-800-288-4677)

The views expressed in this work are solely those of the author and do not necessarily reflect the views of the publisher, and the publisher hereby disclaims any responsibility for them.

ISBN: 978-0-595-52244-6 (pbk)
ISBN: 978-0-595-50993-5 (cloth)
ISBN: 978-0-595-62299-3 (ebk)

Printed in the United States of America

Acknowledgements

Numerous people contributed to the telling of the Captain's story. Most of the contributors of anecdotal information are individually identified throughout the story and their assistance is greatly appreciated.

I give thanks and apologize to those folks who provided snippets of information, which may or may not, appear in the text.

My special thanks to Elizabeth Ewald for pointing out the difference between "who is whom," and "whom is who" and putting commas in all the right places.

My very special thanks to Captain Frank and Ann Pabst for accepting me as a friend and thereby enriching my life.

Contents

Introduction

Though not classified as a Great Lake, measured from a historical and scenic viewpoint, Lake Champlain is indisputably one of North America's greatest lakes. Everyone who ventures upon the crystalline blue water of the lake is treated to a panorama so spectacular and beautiful that it inspires poetic description. Huge sentinels in the form of the Green Mountains of Vermont to the east, and the majestic Adirondack Mountains of New York to the west, provide a vista that gives the lake an appearance of unspoiled, wild and rugged beauty. Numerous tree covered islands, rich with history, add to the beauty of this grand body of water and encourage exploration. Adding to the historical glamour of the lake is the unsolved mystery of whether or not a dinosaur-like creature referred to as Champ, or Champy, dwells within the lake's depths.

Uniquely extending from the United States into Canada, Lake Champlain has served as a major water highway on the North American continent since 1609 when French military officer and explorer Samuel de Champlain, explored its waters in a canoe oared by Native Americans. Over the next two centuries, the lake – because of its strategic location and value as a water highway for commerce – would become an arena for many naval battles as nations fought for control of North America. Two particular engagements would prove significant in deciding the fate and future of the United States of America. The first, occurring in 1776, found a small flotilla of poorly armed vessels, under the command of a young revolutionary general by the name of Benedict Arnold, engaging a much larger fleet of well-armed British war vessels in a part of Lake Champlain known as Valcour channel. The

British were victorious in this naval duel, which resulted in the sinking of the American gunboats *Royal Savage* and *Philadelphia*. Ironically, though losing the battle, the ragtag American fleet had succeeded in delaying the British in their push toward Fort Ticonderoga. Needing to rearm and replenish supplies, and fearing the onset of winter, the British fleet withdrew to Canada. This delay gave the Americans a full winter to build a new fleet and bolster their defenses. The second battle, occurring in 1814, took place in Cumberland Bay within sight of the City of Plattsburgh. Once again, an outgunned, overmatched flotilla of American vessels under the command of young Commodore Thomas Macdonough engaged a mighty British armada under the command of Captain George Downie, an experienced naval officer. During the engagement, Downie was killed and a well-placed salvo of cannon fire from the American flagship *Saratoga* severed the anchor from the British frigate *Confiance*. The ship's huge steel anchor dropped into the waters of Champlain and settled into silt at the bottom of the lake. The loss of this anchor prevented the *Confiance* from turning the large vessel so as to fire the battery of cannons on the opposite side of the ship. With her commander mortally wounded and the ship in danger of sinking, the *Confiance* struck her colors. The result was that the remaining British ships and an accompanying large land army retreated to Canada. Historians would subsequently concur that the loss of the *Confiance's* anchor was not only responsible for an American victory, however, even more significantly; was responsible for ending the war and assuring the establishment of a more northern border with Canada.

Approximately 150 years would pass before a modern day explorer by the name of Frank F. Pabst visited Lake Champlain, and immediately enamored by the lake's mystique and beauty, he began exploring its surface and depths to locate historical artifacts and ensure their preservation. Over the course of four decades, Frank Pabst became an acknowledged expert concerning Lake Champlain lore and history. His expertise resulted in numerous guest appearances on radio and television to discuss the historical significance of the lake and the importance of preserving a healthy lake environment. This expertise resulted in his being hired by National Geographic Magazine to conduct underwater research in Lake Champlain.

In 1967, teenagers snorkel diving near the west shore of Cliff Haven – located two miles south of Plattsburgh – discovered a cannon lodged in silt at the bottom of the lake approximately 100 yards off shore. Frank Pabst's marine salvage subsequently recovered two intact cannons, later identified as being of French manufacture, and other artifacts from a French vessel that sunk at the spot in 1759. A controversy erupted over right of recovery and ownership of the cannon, creating an exciting chapter of irony needing to be told.

In 1976, Pabst purchased a boat constructed in 1945, converted it into a tour boat and commenced operation of *Juniper Boat Tours* from property located in the City of Plattsburgh. Passengers aboard the Juniper enjoyed the beauty of Lake Champlain and its islands, while treated by the *Captain* to a narrated history of the lake and its importance to America. *Juniper Boat Tours* would operate for 25 years, providing thousands of passengers a glimpse of Lake Champlain history while appreciating some of the most spectacular scenery in the world. The story of *The Juniper* contributed to making its *Captain* into a living legend of the lake. The story of how a basically simple, enigmatic human being developed into a maker of legend is fascinating, interesting, exciting and a story that should be told and preserved as an inspiration to all mankind.

During the course of 25 years, thousands of visitors to Lake Champlain boarded a vessel more resembling a stout and sturdy tugboat than a pleasure cruise vessel and were greeted by the words, "Ladies and gentlemen, welcome aboard the *Juniper*." Most would forever remember their cruise on Lake Champlain as scenic, breathtakingly beautiful and an eye-opener as to the lake's historical significance in the shaping of the United States of America. They would remember the *Juniper's* Captain, as a man who portrayed great love for the lake and who possessed infinite knowledge of the lake's history. In all likelihood they would describe the *Juniper's* Captain as a man appearing to have been born of the sea and raised at sea. Indeed, the Captain's ruddy complexion, probing blue eyes, thatch of unruly white hair partially hidden beneath a Greek mariner's cap, and the side to side rolling deck walk of a seasoned mariner offered ample evidence to support that belief. They would be surprised to learn that this friendly, salty appearing sea captain destined to become a legend of Lake Champlain was neither born of the sea, nor, indigenous to the

Champlain Valley. In fact, he was hardly aware of the lake's existence until about 22 years of age. Like Samuel de Champlain, the first white man to view the lake in 1609 – and who would become the lake's namesake – the *Captain of the Juniper* discovered the lake because he was an adventurer and entrepreneur seeking new horizons that would provide excitement, adventure and financial gain. The lake met those expectations and provided much more in terms of joy and happiness. In fact, the beautiful lake proved to be a subtle seductress as demanding as a mistress, but neither Frank, nor his wife, cared, for time spent on the lake was happy time.

Ladies and gentlemen, welcome aboard the *Juniper!* You are about to embark on a cruise through the life of a simple man who during a fifty-year love affair with Lake Champlain, significantly contributed to the lake's historical evolvement and in the process – unintended and quite by accident – became a living legend of the lake. This voyage's ports of call (chapters) are arranged to provide every passenger (reader) a wide range of emotional pleasure while cruising over the usually calm, yet sometimes stormy unpredictable sea, that defined your Captain's life. Before 'we' cast off, you are invited to make yourself comfortable and prepare to enjoy your cruise through the life and times of Frank F. Pabst, *Captain of the Juniper.* Cast off!

The Captain's Early Years

Frank Frederick Pabst was born in Brooklyn, New York, on July 7, 1932, the only child of Frank Peter Pabst and Margaret Pabst - nee Foster. Of German heritage, Frank Frederick became the second scion to bear the name Frank, and would later keep the tradition alive by naming his first-born Frank Eric Pabst. Frank Hugo Pabst arrived in the United States from Germany, around the start of the 20th century and, after clearing Ellis Island, settled into a section of New York City consisting mostly of German emigrants. Like the thousands of other immigrants arriving in America in that era, Frank sought to achieve the American dream of freedom, wealth and prosperity in a land that seemed to have an abundant supply of each. Although proud of his German heritage, he was eager to become an American citizen and looked forward to raising his family as Americans. A design engineer, Frank Hugo obtained employment with the Eberhardt-Faber Pencil Company.

The Captain fondly recalls, "My grandfather designed many things that had to do with the manufacture of wooden pencils. He built many machines in his machine shop and many of his designs were patented in his employer's name. The company told him that because he worked for them, those inventions that benefited the manufacture of pencils belonged to them. Perhaps that was so. In any event, my grandfather received no recognition and no royalties from his designs. Sadly, I never got to know Grandfather Pabst well, because he passed away when I was five years old. However, my grandfather from my mother's side of the family and I enjoyed an excellent relationship. My mother's parents, Fred and Barbara Foster, had two sons and three daughters: Helen, Hony, Margaret, Fred and Bill. Like Grandfather

Pabst, Grandfather Foster immigrated to America from Germany. After arriving in America he sought work wherever he could find it in order to support his family and improve their lot in life. Drive and ambition led to his driving a mule team in the desert hauling Borax; he panned for gold in the gold fields and worked at many interesting things to make a living and put food on his family table; however, he had been trained as an iron molder in Germany, and his goal and true ambition was to own his own iron foundry in America. After kicking around the country and working at many menial jobs, granddad managed to save enough money to make his dream come true. He started his own iron foundry business in Brooklyn, and was able to cast many things out of iron. During World War II, Grandfather Foster refused to cast anything that had to do with the war, so while other iron foundry owners got rich during that time of war, he was just able to eke out a living. When old enough, sons Bill and Fred joined their father's business. They began to specialize in forging bronze and aluminum products, for which there was a big demand, and they started making some serious money. The business kept expanding and eventually it consisted of two city blocks. Grandfather Foster had a Henderson motorcycle with a sidecar attached. When I visited him in Brooklyn we'd get up at 4:00 a.m. and ride through Brooklyn on the motorcycle. He would stop at a *Bickford's restaurant*, buy me a big breakfast, and then we went to Coney Island. He watched the sun come up over the ocean while I played on the beach. I had a great time with my grandfather and he was an outstanding man. I was told that Grandfather's foundry burned down in 1929, and with help from the Masons – and others – he rebuilt it. He paid everybody off and had a successful business going when he passed away at the age of 85. Unfortunately, the way it worked in those days his sons inherited everything. They quickly sold the business and went into retirement. My mother and her sisters got very little from the estate.

My father, Frank Peter Pabst, obtained employment with Consolidated Edison Power Company and continued employment with them until his retirement, which sadly he didn't get to enjoy much of because he passed away at the age of 65. My mother Margaret was a devoted housewife, remaining silent in most family matters; however, when illness or tragedy struck our family, or things weren't going well, she placed whatever personal emotions she was experiencing in check and rallied us to be strong, get past the trauma and move on with our lives. I would say that my Mom epitomizes the ruggedness and stoical makeup of her Teutonic heritage and lived a long life, passing into the hands of our Lord at the age of 98."

The name Pabst immediately invokes the thought of a popular American beer, causing one to wonder if the New York City Pabst's were related to the beer brewing family of wealth and fame that settled in the Midwest. Throughout life Frank has been asked that question many times and his droll response is the sort of answer one could expect from a man with smiling blue eyes that display a hint of mischief. "My stock answer is, there is no blood relationship that is known; however, during my lifetime I have made significant contributions to the Pabst Brewing family's wealth, which should permit me to claim relationship either by consumption or osmosis."

Frank proudly states, "Minus any formal education, my dad earned an unlimited refrigeration license from New York City and became a borough supervisor for Con. Ed., supervising 18 locations in Queens and 4 in the Bronx.

After I was born my parents left Brooklyn and we moved into my grandparents home located just off Horace Harding Boulevard in Flushing Queens. They had a large house so there was plenty of room for us. My grandparent's home was situated on top of a hill overlooking a marsh that would later become the location of the 1939-40 New York World's Fair. One of my earliest memories is the thump, thump, thump of steam pile drivers hammering all night long. Those pile drivers were driving piles into a swamp called Flushing Meadows, which is located between Flushing and Corona, Queens. It was quite exciting for me – as a young lad – to see this section of marshland being converted into something of such significance. The conversion of what amounted to an unusable, worthless swamp into a magnificent exhibition visited by perhaps a couple million people was truly amazing! I consider myself an optimist, and in all likelihood, witnessing the conversion of that marsh as a young child, aided my lifelong belief that anything is possible if one has the ambition and desire and works hard enough to achieve it."

Frank admits to being somewhat of a rebel and renegade in his youth, "but I was never really bad, evil or malicious. I was just somewhat of a free spirit wanting to have fun. I get bored real easy and school was real boring. I performed well enough in school, passed every test I took and in fact aced most of them, but I had trouble focusing on doing homework and enjoyed participating in pranks. Those two things got me into trouble. Even at an early age, I had restless feet. There was a big world out there waiting for me and I wanted to start exploring it. I thought school was a waste of time, and I could be making better use of my time making money, so I started skipping school when I was about 11 and stopped going to school when I was about 13 years old. My parents didn't pressure me about school and I don't believe any sort of official notification was provided the school that I was dropping out. The best way to describe what happened is that school and I just parted company. Neither of my parents had received much formal education so they didn't hassle me about getting an education. They did not see the worth of a school diploma and were proponents of 'learning by doing' and earning your way through life. They just insisted that I be responsible and productive. I suppose in today's world a kid being raised the way I was would be considered as being neglected, abused, having attention deficit disorder or hauled into court as a kid in need of supervised discipline. But there wasn't anything wrong with me. I was just fiercely independent and wanted to strike out on my own."

In continued reflection on a recalcitrant youth, Frank relates, "We moved to College Point when I was about 7 years old. College Point is a point in the East River where the river enters Long Island Sound. Our home was located just below the Bronx-Whitestone Bridge. The headquarters for Ira S. Bushey, who was a major force in the New York City tugboat business - in that day – bordered our back lawn. Bushey owned a fleet of tugs that hauled sludge from the Tallman Island sewer plant located just down the street from our house – out to sea. He also owned a fleet of tugs known as the Red Star Line. In those days the city saw nothing wrong with dumping garbage at sea but in later years it was determined to be bad for the marine environment and I believe the practice has been stopped. After we moved to College Point, I hung around the water a lot and being an inquisitive kid, I explored the many rotting hulks of partially sunken boats and barges with my friends. We established a clubhouse in the cabin of a canal barge that was in a group of partially submerged barges that had been intentionally sunk to create a breakwater. We had some great times in that clubhouse. To me our clubhouse was like a James Bond secret rendezvous place because we could row a rowboat through a hole in the side of the barge and tie up at the bottom of the cabin/clubhouse that was above water. Our clubhouse had three levels: one level 3-4 feet above deck, a second level located about 4 feet below deck and another below that. We tied our boats up at the lowest level, and then climbed into the upper levels. We stocked our clubhouse with a lot of stuff and we even had a hand-crank Victrola for playing records. Minus the availability of a rowboat, our clubhouse could be accessed from land but it was tricky, difficult and dangerous. The reason was that the breakwater had been created at a time when wooden river barges were being phased out. Not knowing what else to do with them, the owners tied them together, smashed holes in their side to partially sink them and thereby created an effective breakwater. A lot of the barges had been there for 20 or 30 years and their timbers were quite rotten so we had to know where to step to avoid smashing through those rotted boards. I had some wonderful playmates, we had a great clubhouse and it was a very happy time in my life. Our clubhouse was also a business office of sorts, because, even as kids we were always looking for ways to make money. In the fall season we scooped up clams and sold them by the bushel to local taverns. We were doing quite well at this enterprise until one of our club members became real clever and decided we could steal the bushel of clams sold to one tavern and then sell the hot clams to another tavern. This was quite profitable until we got caught. For a time we walked around bearing the imprint of a foot that kicked our rear ends and we had difficulty sitting down."

The Young Mariner

Life was never dull or boring for young Frank because he had numerous playmates, and felt fortunate to live within a stone's throw – well, maybe several stones throw – of Long Island Sound. Even in the 1930's there were a lot of people in College Point, but at times it seemed the ever-present swarm of seagulls were more numerous than people. Frank enjoyed watching the gulls swoop, dive and squabble over morsels of food and thrilled at the sound of their shrill cacophony. Perhaps it was this friendship with the gulls, aided and abetted by the lulling sound of a gentle surf kissing the shores of Flushing Bay or Powell Cove, that inspired the boy destined to achieve legendary status as an underwater explorer, marine salvage operator and lake tour boat Captain to go to sea. Admittedly this whimsical thought comes from the mind of the author. The practical truth is that Frank was inspired by a strong desire for independence, excitement, and earning money. Working as a crewman on a river ship at age 11, development of a sunken ship's pilothouse into a teenage clubhouse, and diving into the hold of a sunken tea schooner at the age of 13, fulfilled those needs. The telling of the tea schooner dive reveals it was a foolhardy stunt and flew contrary to the safety and procedures Frank would provide diving enthusiasts in later years.

"Hey, I was young, reckless and foolish when I did it," Frank states with a chuckle as he begins the reflection. "When I started diving I did what a lot of other people did at that time. I had a 5gallon syrup can with a window cemented into it on my head. There was a small air hose attached to the can and to a pump up above. The diver had to rely on the guy operating the hand pump, not to stop to wipe his brow. My first dive was into the hold of a sunken tea schooner that was in back of my house in College Point. I went down with a couple of flat irons tied to a rope around my waist. The hold of the boat was filled with scrap steel and had been intentionally run aground so it would become a breakwater. To us kids, it was a gorgeous boat and we named her *'Jeanie.'* If you follow 122nd street in College Point, due west toward Chisholm Park, you can still see what's left of the *'Jeanie.'* That was my first diving experience. If the guy on the pump didn't pump fast enough, the water level inside the homemade helmet started to rise and, minus gills, the diver would drown."

In today's society it seems incredible that anyone would employ an 11year old child as a crew hand on a ship, but Frank was a child in an era that not only permitted, but expected, children to begin working for their own income.

"I consider myself fortunate for having spent my youth in an era where child labor and child safety laws were practically nonexistent, and it wasn't as if, as an 11yr. old, I answered an employment application. My starting on the tugs could be compared to the kid who goes to his neighbors and asks if he can mow their lawn, rake leaves or shovel their sidewalk. I hung around the waterfront a lot and was fascinated by the tugs. I got to know a lot of people who worked on the tugboats and my dad knew a lot of them too. One day he told me that if I wanted to go out on a tug, I could. It was during World War II, I was eleven years old, and most men were off doing things connected with the war - so 'hands' on the tugs were in demand. I started working on a tugboat during my summer vacation and made good money. When fall came I started missing a lot of school, because I preferred working on the tugboat and making money. My deckhand title was Oiler and my job was to keep various points on the tug's engine lubricated with oil. There were little cups in several locations on the engine and I had to keep those cups filled. A working tugboat engine required a lot of oil. The first tugboat that I worked on was a steam driven tug and the temperature would get well over 100 degrees in the engine room. It was hot, dirty work causing my body to be constantly soaked with sweat. Water oozed out of every pore. I was constantly thirsty and therefore was hitting the water bucket much of the time. There was a big Swedish guy working on the tug and he shoveled six tons of coal into the boiler on a watch.

Swede saw me consuming a lot of water and asked, "What's the matter kid, is your mouth dry?"

"Very dry," I responded.

"He handed me a wad of chewing tobacco that had been soaked in rum and said, 'here try this, it will cut down the need for water.'

I took the wad, inserted it in my mouth, behind my lip, and it gave me a good feeling. I was quite pleased and told myself, *here I am only 11 years old and I'm flying with the big boys.* Well, I had this cud in my mouth and we were cruising down the Hudson River with two sand scows in tow. I went up on deck to throw some ashes overboard. I was standing on the edge of the deck, with one foot on the rail watching the piers lining Manhattan pass by. The big Swede who had given me the tobacco was off watch. He came quietly up behind me and smacked me on the back. The blow startled me and I swallowed the cud. By the time the tobacco reached my stomach I had turned green and felt horrible. I was instantly sick to my stomach, and for a time, I could shit through the eye of a needle and not hit the sides. That was the first and last time I touched chewing tobacco. I enjoyed working on the tugs, was making good money, had no desire to go to school, so I stopped going by the time I turned 13."

Venturing into the big water of the ocean during a time when German U-boats were hunting America's coastal waters was exciting for the young crewman and recalled as an enjoyable and memorable experience.

"The tug I worked on didn't confine its work to New York harbor. We made some coastal trips hauling barges filled with oil and gasoline up to Greenland. Barges didn't sit in the water as deep as tankers, so they presented a more difficult target to hit by torpedoes fired from a U-boat. Life was exciting and enjoyable during that period of my youth and I learned a great deal about ships, the engines that drove them, and the navigation required to get from point A to point B."

Landlubber

Having reached the ripe old age of 16, restless feet, the desire for adventure and lure of money caused Frank to leave the tugs and become a landlubber.

"When I was on shore, I met up with a guy who drove trucks. He took me for a ride in his truck, let me drive it, and that got me interested in trucks. Soon after taking that ride, I obtained employment with H.G. Rose Moving and Storage Company as a truck driver. H.G. Rose was initially chartered to National Van Lines located at Blue Island, Chicago, and later sold to Howard Van Lines. It was necessary for my employer to sign on with those big companies in order to use their interstate hauling rights. I got this job just as the war was ending and a lot of military and former military were being transferred all over the country. It was a busy time for furniture moving companies. Typical of government, a lot of the moves didn't make sense and seemed a waste of money to me. For example, I moved a naval officer and his family from Boston to San Diego, returning to New York, via Omaha, Nebraska, where I picked up a load for New York. I then took another load to San Diego and was assigned to pick up the furnishings of the same naval officer we had moved only a few weeks before and take them back to Boston. It cost the government $6000 to move that guy from Boston to San Diego and back to Boston again. When I started work for the company, I was assigned a 22-foot stake rack truck to drive and on a trip upstate, I wrecked the truck. What happened was that I lost the brakes on the truck just after topping a hill on Route 17 - somewhere near Middletown, New York. There was a diner in the middle of that hill. I went off the road, through the kitchen of the diner and eventually came to a stop against a tree. It was a pretty bad wreck and fortunately no one was seriously injured. I took the kitchen off the diner and my truck was totaled including most of my load. Luckily, I walked away from that with only minor scrapes and pains. My employer didn't fault me for the accident and when I got back to New York City, I was given a KB International Tractor, which pulled a 28-foot trailer to drive. This truck had vacuum over hydraulic brakes, whereas the straight job that I wrecked had just hydraulic brakes.

My boss explained and asked, 'Eddie was supposed to take this load to Chicago, but he got drunk and can't go. Do you think you can drive this rig to Chicago?'

I had never driven a tractor-trailer but I thought to myself, *'Shucks, I can do this, and it means big bucks.'* I responded, "Sure I can, it's just like the other truck I drove except it bends in the middle. Well, I left New York and headed for Chicago, and it was an exciting trip because as previously mentioned, I had never driven a tractor-trailer before. Everything went along fine until I ran into a detour outside of Chicago. I misread the sign for the detour and got on the wrong road. It was a narrow road and I was about a mile up the road before realizing my mistake. There was no place to turn the rig around so, I had to back out of the road. It took me 3 hours to back the rig that one-mile. If any tractor-trailer drivers witnessed my struggle that day, they were provided a good laugh and are probably still telling their grandchildren the story about the kid driver who didn't have a clue as to how to back up a rig. I would back up about 50-feet, then had to drive forward 25-feet to straighten out again. Actually, it was a good thing this happened to me because by the time I got out of that dilemma, I knew the rudiments of backing up a trailer and was quite proficient at it from that time on. My employment for the moving company resulted in my driving a tractor-trailer through every state in the continental U.S. before I was 17-years old. Eventually, I graduated to driving a White Tractor, which had a factory built sleeper cab. This truck was wrecked on a trip south and the circumstances are rather interesting. It was around two in the morning. I was in low gear climbing a steep mountain located near Rogersville, Tennessee. A bootlegger driving a '41 Chevrolet truck loaded with hooch was coming down the mountain toward me. He lost control of his vehicle and ended up under the axle of the White. His front wheels wound up under the dolly wheels on our trailer. The Chevrolet was demolished and the bootlegger was killed instantly. Fortunately, my co-driver and I were not injured; however, the load of moonshine spilled over a wide area and made a stinking mess. After that accident, I was assigned to drive a four-cylinder GM diesel and made many trips to the west coast with it. Of course I was always after more money so while working for the moving company, I applied for work as a steeplejack, was hired, and ended up working for both United Steeplejack and Empire Steeplejack. I worked with a crew that placed the television antennas on the Empire State building. The magnificent vista observed from atop the building made this job an enjoyable experience. Far below, the streets were filled with cars that looked like large bugs roaming about in search of escape from the vast concrete maze that entrapped them. The thousands of people on the sidewalks, crossing streets and entering or exiting buildings resembled ants exiting or entering many concrete anthills. Looking south, the sight of Lady Liberty's arm stretched skyward displaying the torch of Liberty made me proud to be an American. From atop the tallest building in New York City, (World Trade Center was yet to be built) the Harlem and East Rivers looked like tiny brooks and the mighty Hudson seemed narrower than it did when I cruised its surface on tugs; however, the bustling activity at the many docks lining the west side of Manhattan Island and number of vessels arriving and departing were indicative of the Hudson's importance to the economy of – not only New York – but the nation. Looking north toward Harlem, a large green expanse in the center of an otherwise concrete maze defined Central Park, and in the distance the magnificent George Washington Bridge connecting New York to New Jersey, resembled a tinker toy set in place by some kid. Looking northeast toward the Bronx, Yankee Stadium seemed like some sort of Roman Coliseum surrounded on all sides by high-rise tenements that I knew were home to thousands of immigrants from many different countries of the world. From atop the magnificent edifice I could identify the boundaries of the city's many ethnic communities. Each community had sprung from the need and desire of newcomers to feel more secure and comfortable living among people who spoke the same language, held the same customs and followed the same culture, while slowly assimilating into this great nation called America. Irish, Italian, German, Polish, Jewish, Chinese, Hispanic, and Blacks, clustered together in specific sections of the city, and each section – by the time I was a young man

– was more readily identified by its ethnic name than the borough of the city that it occupied. From atop the Empire State building, I could readily identify those sections of the city referred to as Black Harlem, Spanish Harlem, Little Italy, Chinatown, Germantown, etc. Looking east and southeast toward Queens and Brooklyn, I could see the Bronx-Whitestone Bridge and pinpoint the location of my home in relation to it. Needless to say, I really enjoyed working on that job. With tongue in cheek I would add that while up top I looked for ape hair and dried piles of gorilla turd but didn't find any. I guess the folks at RKO cleaned things up real good after King-Kong made his historic climb up the building holding gorgeous Fay Wray.

While working as a steeplejack I was part of a crew that had the task of painting all the flagpoles in the New York City school system, and there were quite a few. I was quite agile in my youth and could scale a 100-foot flagpole in nothing flat. Quite naturally, our crew was always looking for ways to make our job easier. One thing that we did – that would come back to bite us – had to do with the gold ball atop every flagpole. Our contract called for removing the ball from every pole. After the ball was removed gold leaf was applied to it and then the ball was re-attached to the top of the pole. We decided that folks standing on the ground couldn't tell the difference between gold leaf and gold paint and we could speed up the process by just applying gold paint to the ball while it was attached to the pole. Then we got the even brighter idea that if we just painted the bottom of the ball no one would know. We didn't realize that the inspector for the school system would fly over the tops of the poles in a plane to inspect our work. That is what happened, and we were ordered to go back and repaint all the poles. It was necessary to repaint the entire pole after they were climbed, so we couldn't just redo the gold balls. The poles were climbed through the use of two straps attached to the climber and flagpole. We hiked our way up the pole by moving the straps. We also cleaned the flues in the Waldorf Astoria Hotel, and that was an interesting adventure. It was a nasty job! We had to lower ourselves down the flues and clean out the grease that accumulated. We also replaced the Cornish on a building that had broken off during a windstorm. We worked on that by using a block and tackle and pulling ourselves up while seated in a boatswain chair. I also was part of a steeplejack crew that replaced the slate roof on Wards Island Mental Hospital. Our zeal to speed up this job ended up costing either our company, or the state, a lot of additional money. Actually it was the boss of our crew who came up with the brilliant time and labor saving measure that we employed, so he ended up taking the heat for what happened. This is that story: the old slate roof had to be removed before we installed new slate. For the task of removal, we constructed a barrier/bulkhead at the edge of the roof. We then knocked the old slate loose and it slid down the roof and up against the bulkhead. The slate was then placed in five gallon pails, which when full, were lowered to the ground. It was a slow process because tons of slate strained against the bulkhead and needed to be lowered to the ground.

After a few hours of using the bucket to ground – bucket back to roof – process, our boss told us, "I'm going to take the inspector to lunch. While we're gone, knock out the props holding the bulkhead and let the slate fall to the ground."

"We did as directed and in the process the approximately 20-tons of slate falling from the roof broke 144 windows in the building. The old slate was all on the ground when the boss and inspector returned from lunch but a lot of broken glass was mixed in with the pile. I don't know what happened to the boss on that job, but I didn't see him on any more jobs."

Working part time as a truck driver and part time as a steeplejack didn't produce enough excitement or money for young Frank, so in 1948, the 16year old obtained another part time job as a tow-truck operator for Blue Bird Towing in Whitestone, New York.

Frank recalls, "Blue Bird had a franchise to provide towing service for a 35-mile stretch of the Belt Parkway from Northern Boulevard up to the Sunrise Highway. They might have had a larger area, but that was the section I used to cover. The company owned 15 tow trucks and I drove a 1948 Chevrolet truck that had a hand winch. I worked on a salary plus commission, receiving a commission on whatever bodywork we managed to sell. Several exciting things happened while I was driving a tow truck and one incident that is forever etched in my memory remains questionable as to whether what I saw was an accident or suicide. One afternoon I was parked on the grass adjacent to the northbound lane of the Belt Parkway by Fort Totten, and I saw this Dodge coming up real fast. I watched as it veered off the road nice and straight driving directly into a concrete bridge abutment. The car was

13

instantly transformed into a pile of bent and twisted metal and broken glass. I drove up behind the wreck, got out of my truck and went to check on the driver's condition. The driver's head – or what was left of it – was pinned between the back of the seat and the steering wheel. It was a horrible sight! The poor fellow had been decapitated and there was blood everywhere. I went back to my truck, got on the radio and reported the crash to my dispatcher. I then got out of my truck and wretched! That was a long time ago, but I'll never forget it."

Although not scholastically ambitious, no one would ever accuse Frank of lacking ambition for he was always looking for work that would improve his income and his lot in life. As already evidenced, during his youth he worked at many menial jobs that provided a meager income, all the while harboring the desire to start his own business. Knowing that could not happen until he had some capital for investment, he accepted employment wherever he could, working both day and night, so that he could salt some money away. However, saving was not easy for a young man who enjoyed partying, and who freely lavished money on friends.

"During and after The War," Frank explains, "there was a lot of employment. I was too young to be drafted into the military and I drifted from one job to another. I went from working on the tugs to driving truck, became a member of a steeplejack crew and tow truck operator, all the while continuing to look for ways I could make more money. In that endeavor I managed to get a job driving taxi for 'Wags Transportation Company' and worked for Mike Greco. Wags was a yellow cab company in the city and Mike operated a call-in cab service for them in Flushing. Although our cabs worked out of an office in Flushing, we went to Manhattan, Brooklyn, the Bronx, wherever we were called. At the same time I was a cabbie, I went to work as a diver for 'Merritt-Chapman-Scott' a rigging outfit. There was nothing romantic or interesting about that underwater experience, because mostly my work consisted of descending into dark, heavily polluted water to repair hull damage on tankers, which was not pleasant work. I kept myself busy. If I had work in one area fine, if not, I'd go back to driving taxi. I drove a 'hack' on and off for several years. The taxi job was a backdoor buffer for me. If I couldn't find work as a steeplejack or diver, I'd go over to Wags and take out a cab. This was before the City required 'hack' licenses. There were only so many taxis allowed in

New York City, and the cab companies operating there were required to purchase a Medallion from the city. Medallions were worth more than the cabs. I saw guys sell a cab having a blown engine for $100,000 because the buyer was purchasing the Medallion that went with it.

During that time of my life I had a lot of part time jobs that were providing a sufficient income but I wanted to become my own boss and own my own business. One of the jobs that I almost forgot to mention was paperboy. I started delivering newspapers around the age of 10, before I went to work on the tugs, and returned to that line of work after leaving the tugboats, just before I got a job driving truck. Selling newspapers was a fun job because it was a group effort by myself, and the kids I hung out with. Every day we went as a group over to Jamaica Station, which was the drop point for bundles of the *Daily News* and *Mirror*. We picked up the bundles, and sold individual copies in front of movie theaters and in various bars. We were able to sell the next day's paper at 9:00 o'clock in the evening and they went like hotcakes. We made some serious money hustling newspapers because we paid 1 cent per copy for the papers and sold them for between 10 cents and 25 cents per paper. But I knew that there was more to life than selling newspapers and was pleased to obtain work driving truck. While driving truck, I learned that Al's Auto Wrecking, a junkyard located on Roosevelt Avenue in Flushing was being sold in a tax sale. I was around 18 or 19 years old, making good money as a trucker, and managed to purchase the business for $2500. My junkyard was located on the site of the present day home of the New York Mets, known as Shea Stadium. At the time, there were 10 junkyards on Roosevelt Avenue, the other 9 were owned by Italian Americans and I was the only non-Italian owned business in that area. I realize that immediately triggers thoughts of the Mafia or an organized effort by those Italian competitors to run me out and take over my business, but that did not happen and we got along just fine. I had a couple of 'gentlemen' (hey, just because they drank a lot and might have been busted a couple of times doesn't mean they weren't gentlemen) working for me in the yard. We dismantled cars, salvaging radiators, alternators and parts that we could sell, and the rest of the car went into scrap. In those days, after you cut the engine out of a car for cast iron, and got all of the steel out of it, the frame was cut into sections of steel. When we got through, all that was left was the car's body. We disposed of the car bodies by giving them to the Italian yard owners, who hauled them over to New Jersey and sold them to a recycler of tin. They hauled the bodies on stake rack trucks over to Jersey, and as they could only carry about 4 in each load, they made just enough money to pay for their gas, and not much else, even though at the time gasoline was 19-cents a gallon. I hadn't been in business long when I learned that the city wanted 5 water towers torn down and was putting the razing of them out for bid. I offered a bid that was $5000 less than the next lowest bidder and got the job. My competitors were scratching their heads wondering how I would be able to do the work and make money on it. The answer was simple: the towers had been examined by all of the bidders and they were all locked into the same antiquated, costly mode of removal. Their plan called for erecting scaffolding around the towers and leasing a crane to haul down the steel plate. My plan eliminated the need for scaffolding and the leasing of an expensive crane. I went down to the Brooklyn Navy Yard, and purchased a balsa wood raft that had once been on a Liberty ship. I hoisted the raft to the top of each tank, along with my cutting torches. Then we flooded the tank, drained the water down about two inches, cut the top out of the tower and placed the raft in the tank. Then while working from the raft, we lowered the water in 5-foot increments, cutting down steel plate in sections that were lowered inside and to the bottom of the tank. We repeated the process gradually reducing each tank into manageable size steel plates. This method permitted me to do the work at a fraction of what it would have cost my competitors using their method. I made enough money on that job to buy two flatbed trailers and a Brockway tractor. I also bought a car-crusher press. This permitted us to place a car in the crusher and compact it into a 3-foot cube. After purchasing the crusher, I started purchasing all the tin and car bodies from the other junkyards on Roosevelt Ave; after it was pressed into cubes, we hauled the cubes over to New Jersey on the flatbed trailers. In 1951, my junkyard business was thriving and money was rolling in. I was 19years old and thought I had found my niche in life. Then out of the blue, I received a surprise and it was an offer I couldn't refuse. It was an offer to become a member of America's armed forces, which were engaged in a new war on a God-forsaken peninsula that went by the name of Korea."

Drafted

"Although there was little doubt in most Americans minds that our country was at war, our nations politicians did not refer to it as a war, instead calling it a 'Military Action,' which I suppose made our presence there seem more acceptable. The draft notice directed me to report to the U.S. Army Induction Center in Manhattan, on December 11th, 1951, for induction into the U.S. Army. The draft notice came at a horrible time because I was making good money and my business was worth around $200,000. However, being a patriotic citizen, and fully realizing that failure to appear could land my ass in jail, I put my business up for sale and prepared to report for induction. Wouldn't you know, at the same time, the price of steel took a whack, forcing me to sell for much less than the business was worth. I auctioned off everything I owned and cleared about $5,000 from the sale. Still, I was thankful, because it could have been worse. Five thousand bucks was a nice sum of money in 1951. To this day I still have an inclination toward the junk business, and during the years I operated my lake salvage business from the Plattsburgh waterfront, some of my detractors accused me of operating a junkyard because of all the equipment I stored on my property. To them it might have looked like junk, but most of it was material and equipment I used in the salvage end of my business."

Although realizing that upon completion of military indoctrination, he would be sent to Korea, Frank accepted the assignment as 'just another adventure in life' and started seeking ways to make the most of it. His experience as a truck driver and knowledge of trucks, landed him a job driving a 'deuce and a half' in convoys that hauled ammunition and other supplies, up to the front lines.

"I went over to Korea and was assigned as a driver in a supply convoy. I was promoted to Sergeant 1st Class after only about 2months, because all the guys senior to me had either rotated out or were killed. Great grub wasn't readily available in the God-forsaken country, and we subsisted mostly on K rations. One of our K ration entrees consisted of beans and sausage. Believe it or not, I actually liked them. One of the guys told me that the beans would taste a lot better if they were heated up, and we could heat them by placing them on the manifold of our trucks. While on convoy, we'd take a break about every hour and during one break, I placed a tin of beans on my truck's manifold, figuring that by the time we took our next break they would be nicely heated. I had just completed placing the beans on my truck's manifold when we came under fire. We were ordered to keep driving and were not allowed to stop for another break. I was driving along and suddenly heard loud exploding noises in the front of my truck. At first I thought my truck had been hit by enemy fire but the truck kept going and I realized it was the sound of exploding beans. What a mess! I had to clean my truck when I got back to the motor pool. About two weeks after that incident, I was in a convoy and a mortar round struck the road just in front of my truck. It blew a section of road away and my truck rolled off the road and down a steep hill. I wound up with some fractured ribs and a lot of bumps and bruises. I considered myself very lucky though, because my truck was loaded with munitions and they didn't explode. I was sent to a hospital located on the island of Iwo Jima, and after a short time there, transferred to a hospital in Kure, Japan. On arrival in Japan, I drew my liquor rations and wanting to see some of the countryside, rented a motorcycle. Kure was only a short distance from Hiroshima, so four other guys and myself decided to visit the city destroyed by an A bomb in 1945. Three American soldiers and a British soldier who were in the same hospital ward were my companions. We had been told that memories of the devastation caused by the atomic bomb were a sensitive issue to the residents and they didn't appreciate the antics of drunken, sex-starved American GI's. It had been a long time since my companions and I had stepped foot in a gin mill or enjoyed the company of the opposite sex, so naturally, we let that advice go in one ear and out the other. By the time we arrived in Hiroshima we had consumed our liquor rations and we were feeling no pain. Inebriation inhibited wisdom and common sense causing us to behave with reckless abandon. I suppose our behavior was inexcusable but, hey, we were young men with raging libidos, on leave from the trauma of combat, looking for a good time and in need of releasing a lot of pent up angry emotion. On arrival in Hiroshima, we drove our motorcycles inside a bar that – unfortunate for us – was filled with MP's, AP's, SP's and just about every military police type you could imagine. Our grand entrance caused a brawl and we ended up getting busted. I probably should have been concerned, but I wasn't. I thought, *'what the hell, the worst that could happen is getting sent back to Korea.'* That is precisely what happened. Except the Army operates in very strange ways. I returned to Korea not as a truck driver but a photographer for CID (Criminal Investigative Division). This assignment seemed stupid to me because I possessed only minimal knowledge of photography. However, everything went along just fine until I got drunk and blew a photo assignment. That incident cost me my stripes and I was transferred to the motor pool. Eventually, I got my stripes back and was promoted to Sergeant First Class. While I was a photographer for CID, I was given some interesting assignments. On one occasion, I photographed a fatal streetcar/pedestrian accident, because witnesses made the allegation that American soldiers in a jeep had forced the 'old papa-san' (elderly Korean male) in front of the streetcar. The old fellow's robe caught on the streetcar and he was pulled under the wheels. It took the streetcar a long time to stop and body parts were scattered for about a mile. I was required to take a photo of every body part and it wasn't pleasant. I was also ordered to photograph an orderly room where a homicide occurred. Three black soldiers had been in the room shooting dice and they got arguing over thirty-seven cents. One soldier left the room, got his carbine, returned to the room and dumped two, 15round clips into the other two guys in the room. That room was just a little bit larger than a broom closet. The Provost Marshall ordered me to photograph the entrance holes and exit holes of the victims' wounds. That was easier said than done, because there were so many, it was like trying to photograph a pile of hamburger.

The last six months of my tour in Korea I was placed in charge of the distribution of rations. This proved profitable, because I swapped a lot of stuff around for the right price and acquired some souvenirs to take home with me.

When I received word that I was being shipped home for discharge, I decided to take a few of my acquisitions home with me and I sold the rest. I hid a Russian 'burp gun' in the bottom of my duffle bag and had a 'Mama-san' sew up the bottom of the bag to conceal it. I had also obtained a 1911 chrome plated .45 from an officer in a 'swap' for some stuff, and a .25 Beretta that I usually carried in my waistband. I got rid of most of my clothes, placed the guns in the bag and filled the remaining space in the bag with oranges. I took just enough clothes to get back to the states. A buddy and myself sat up for two nights and used syringes to fill the oranges with vodka and gin. After we got on the boat, we started eating oranges and nobody could figure out why we were looped all the time. One day a Captain I had served with joined me atop a hatch cover and pulled an orange out of my bag. The Captain opened up the orange, tasted it and said, "Aha, that's where you get the hooch!" He seized my bag of oranges that also contained the guns. The booze filled oranges were no big deal but when they discovered what was in the bottom of the bag I was in serious trouble. When we arrived in Seattle, two days later, I was given a summary court martial. I had boarded the boat as a Sergeant 1st class and got off the boat as a Corporal. It didn't bother me that much though because I hadn't planned on making the Army my career. I was discharged on November 11th, 1954, and was happy to return to civilian life."

Return To New York

After bidding farewell to the Army, Frank returned to New York City, to search for employment and new adventure. What he found was that his old neighborhood had changed drastically. Many of the families that he had grown up with in a section of Queens referred to as Germantown had moved and the environment now seemed a lot different and not as pleasant to the returning war veteran.

Frank recalls, "I did not see anything I liked anymore and I felt like a stranger in my own community. My mother and father were still living in their home in College Point, but they were not pleased with the changes occurring in the community either. I contacted my old boss, Mike Greco, at Wags Taxi and was immediately hired to begin driving taxi. Driving a cab was always interesting because almost every fare produced a new personality and a new challenge. However within a month after my return to civilian life one fare proved so challenging that it convinced me to give up driving cab and seek out a less hostile environment in which to live."

Frank's blue eyes and friendly, radiant oval face take on a rare coldness when he describes the events of December 10th 1954. "That night at about 4:30 a.m. I picked up a fare on 8th Avenue in Manhattan. This fare was a very large black male who got into my cab and sat in the jump seat. (A jump seat was a little folding seat located in back of the driver. It was attached to the rear of the front seat and could be raised or lowered as needed.) The fact that he selected the jump seat to sit in made me immediately uncomfortable, and I became a lot more uncomfortable when he told me to just drive up 8th Ave. and he would tell me where to stop when he was ready. He also seemed excited or hopped up on something. I started driving and suddenly, he leaned over the seat and placed a knife against my throat. He told me that he wanted all of my money and if I didn't hand it over, he would slice me from ear to ear. The guy's actions convinced me that whether I gave him my money or not was of little consequence, because he was going to cut my throat anyway. I immediately went into survival mode and started thinking of what I could do to survive. I kept a jack handle under my seat for protection, but I knew that if I suddenly reached down, he would cut my throat. I was driving a 1947 DeSoto with no shocks on it and a plan began to take shape in my mind. When I reached 57th street the light turned red. I jammed on the brakes, and the sudden stop impelled both of us forward. Then I whipped the car into 1st gear and punched it, yanking the hand brake up at the same time. My move caught the robber by surprise and he was thrown forward and backwards in the rear seat. However, I was ready for it and as the cab came to a stop, I took a tuck and roll out of the door and took the lug wrench with me. The black guy opened the door and started to get out bringing his knife arm out first. I hit his arm with the lug wrench and broke the arm. As he continued getting out, I broke his other arm. Then I went to work on him and when I was through it took about 50 stitches to sew his head up. I'm beating the hell out of him and four or five other cabbies come by and at the same time a policeman pulls up.

The cop asks, "What's going on?"'

One of the other cab drivers responded, "That, black guy had a knife and he tried to rob a cabby.'"

The cop yelled back, "Is that the cabbie wielding the tire iron?"'

"Yeah." The same cabbie responded.

"'Well, let me know when he gets tired," the cop replied.'

Of course that was the early 50's and there wasn't much compassion for black men, especially when they were committing a robbery. I was lucky that night, but I wasn't sure how long my luck would last while driving a hack, so I decided to seek other employment and move someplace where there was peace and quiet."

Call of the North Country

"The city of my birth, had been the source of much joy to me in my youth," Frank explained, "but as an adult I saw it in a totally different perspective. Crime ran rampant throughout the city, gangs of young toughs extorted money from businesses and residents feared for their safety. Somewhere between my hitch in the army and return home, the once friendly and trust worthy environment had done a 180 and become an environment of paranoia, fear and distrust. There was so much crime occurring the cops couldn't keep up with it. George McQueen – a good friend who grew up with me, and whom I considered more like a brother than friend – had an uncle in the New York City Police Department. His name was Abbott Bradford and he was a Sergeant in the NYPD Vice Squad. I told George about my close encounter with the robber and expressed that I was fed up with the city and thought it was time to seek out a quieter and safer environment. George told me that his uncle had retired from the PD and moved to a quiet little village up in the Adirondack Mountains, where he and his wife owned and operated a Bed and Breakfast. George invited me to accompany him up to his uncle's for a visit. I had never heard of the community named Elizabethtown, and George described it as located in the Adirondack Mountains, very near Lake Champlain. When he added that Elizabethtown was a beautiful, peaceful, quiet country village, where one could hunt, fish, hike the mountains, or just relax and enjoy retirement, it sounded like just the environment I wanted to live in. When I told my friend I was eager to see the place, he called his uncle and a short time after that I was on my way north with George. The guy tried to rob me on December 10th, and around December 15th, I traveled to Elizabethtown with my friend. I had a great time and fell in love with the place! I returned to New York City after Christmas, but the following Spring I packed up my things and moved to E-town. I was glad I did, and have never regretted leaving the city that would become warmly referred to as 'The Big Apple.' What a joke that was. The closest resemblance New York City has to an apple would be a big rotten one. I was very happy to escape the culture of crime, greed and corruption that had taken over the city of my birth. I used what little money I had saved to purchase a home located between New Russia and Elizabethtown, and went to work as a mechanic at Johnson Chevrolet in Elizabethtown. My most memorable experience from that employment was that I was given the privilege of prepping and delivering the Chevrolet Corvette that Johnny Padres got for getting the winning run for the Dodgers in the 1955 World Series. Shortly after buying my first home and making the down payment, I learned there were so many liens against the property that I would never be able to obtain title to it, so I started looking for another place. I bought a new pickup truck from my employer and to increase my income, hired out as a driver to the Post Office. At the end of my workday at the garage, I drove over to Westport, met the train and picked up the mail for Elizabethtown. On weekends, I obtained work as a handyman, mowing lawns, raking leaves, etc. and that gave me extra money."

Although Frank enjoyed living in Elizabethtown, the quiet little village presented somewhat of a culture shock to a 23-year old, Korean War Veteran from New York City, who had never given much thought to settling down. Until now, work and having a good time had been the only things important to him. A visit to the local ice cream parlor located in the village drugstore was about to change all that.

Love Comes Calling

One hot summer day in 1955 as Frank mopped the sweat from his brow, he decided that ice cream would taste real good and cool him down. This longing called him to the soda fountain at Williams Pharmacy, where he ordered a malted from a young female soda jerk who immediately intrigued him.

"She was a shy, beautiful young woman having sincere friendly eyes and a warm smile. I was immediately smitten."

The look of love radiating from the old Captain's face as he describes his first meeting with the woman who would become his soul mate and wife of 49years, provides ample evidence that he was indeed smitten, and that initial spark ignited a fire of love that grows warmer and brighter with the passage of time. Seeming incredible - after living with a very vocal extrovert for so many years – Ann Elizabeth Duntley Pabst continues to exhibit the same shyness that intrigued the newly arrived young man from the 'city' those many years ago. Shyness aside, as she listens to her husband describe their romance, her face beams brightly in a reciprocal look of love.

"That summer of 1955, I went to the soda fountain at Williams Pharmacy; it was run by a fellow named Frank Stevens, who was a Mason and one of the men who convinced me to become a member of the Masonic Lodge. He had a lovely young lady working at the soda fountain by the name of Ann Duntley. She made an excellent chocolate malted, but her eyes and delightful smile intrigued me far more than the malted. She also was honest and straightforward with me and I would eventually learn that she was the 2nd eldest child in a family of 10 children. Her dad was a hard working dairy farmer who lived an austere life in order to put his children through college.

Her mom was a teacher in a one-room schoolhouse. After marrying, she continued teaching for four years - then stayed home to care for children and help with the farm. The Duntley family lived in a home without running water. They pumped the water they needed from a well. A large cast iron cook stove served double duty, heating the Duntley home and cooking their meals. The austere lifestyle of the Duntley family contributed to Ann's shyness; however, it also instilled her with wonderful qualities of ambition, honesty, integrity and love of family. Her mother instilled the desire to obtain an education that would not only improve her lot in life but improve the quality of life for her family as well. When I walked into that drugstore and met Ann, I didn't realize it at the time, but I found much more than a woman who interested and excited me. In her, I had found the pot of gold at the end of the rainbow, not glittering gold that I could spend, but life-long wealth of love and happiness. I had given up drinking at the time and was pretty straight, and I think she liked that. Anyway, my heart started beating a lot faster when I saw Ann, and I wanted to take her out on a date, but was too shy to ask her myself. I asked Ann's friend, Joanie Bradford, the daughter of the Bradfords who owned a Bed & Breakfast in E-town, to try and set up a date with Ann for me. She was successful and that first date led to many others, one thing led to another, and over the course of that summer romance blossomed. Things were going great between us and then Ann told me that she was going to move to Plattsburgh to attend school. That was a shocker, because I didn't want us to be separated by that distance. I had been in Plattsburgh – just once – back in 1949. I was up there as part of a steeplejack crew that put a roof on the chapel at Clinton Prison. As I recalled, Plattsburgh had not impressed me very much. But, I didn't want to lose Ann, so I rented a small apartment on Pine Street in the City of Plattsburgh and got a job driving fuel truck, delivering fuel to the Plattsburgh Air Force Base. They were just building the base then. During the winter of 1955 the union working on the base went on strike and wouldn't let fuel drivers deliver fuel to the ground control unit that was landing planes at what little airstrip that they had. This problem was overcome by having a military police escort take us onto the base.

Ann attended Plattsburgh State University, while I worked and our relationship kept budding until it blossomed into full flower.

I asked Ann to marry me and she responded that she would be delighted to marry me – right after her eight younger brothers and sisters had completed college! She explained that she felt obligated to aid in supporting them while they were getting their college degrees. That seemed like a frustratingly long wait to me. I pressured her into changing her mind and she agreed to marry me right away. Throughout the winters of 1955-56 I worked for Calso Oil - eventually Chevron Oil - and was making about $75 per week. The local distributor for Calso was Charlie Bonie and I enjoyed working for Charlie; however, that one job wasn't providing me enough income. With the arrival of spring, I went looking for additional employment and was hired to drive an ice cream truck for Sealtest Ice Cream. My boss at Sealtest was a fine gentleman by the name of Bob Hughes, who adhered to many of the ideas and criteria that I use in my life today. Bob had a great personality and was a real gentleman; humble, intelligent, personable, and all of the many great qualities he possessed made him an outstanding human being. Bob provided me a lot of ideas on how to live life and conduct business. Although difficult, I have tried to emulate Bob's business principles throughout my life. I was provided a regular Sealtest delivery route. Each and every workday morning I would drive over to the Sealtest plant in Burlington, pick up a load of ice cream, then return to the Plattsburgh side of the lake and make deliveries to established customers. I enjoyed driving truck for Calso and Sealtest very much; however, Ann had agreed to become my wife, and I realized the need for more income, so with the arrival of the fall season, I set out again looking for work, and got a job as a driver for Bouyea Bakery, which was based in Plattsburgh. I ended up working for the bakery from 1957-67. I started as a relief driver and at first I covered all of the bakery's routes. I eventually wound up taking a route to Lake Placid. When I took over the route it consisted of 13 stops. Through aggressive marketing - in a year's time - I increased it to 112 stops. I managed to turn it into one of the biggest routes that the bakery had. Working both jobs provided me $75-$100 per week.

On January 30, 1957, Ann and I exchanged wedding vows at the Congregational Church in Lewis. The little white wooden church was located on a hill just off Route 9 in the Hamlet of Lewis, and is still there to this day. Lee Bouyea, owner of the bakery I worked for, gave us a very nice wedding cake for our reception, which was held at the home of Ann's aunt Opel, in Westport. It was just a small get together of family and friends. Our honeymoon trip consisted of the drive from Westport to Plattsburgh, but neither of us cared because we were so happy in love, eager to begin the adventure of marriage and eager to start a family. My bride settled into my little 3rd floor apartment located on the corner of U.S. Avenue and McKinley Street in Plattsburgh, and she soon converted what had been a messy bachelor apartment into a neat, clean, cheery home. The apartment wasn't much, but it had a little porch where I could grille hotdogs on a charcoal grille. I was making about $75 per week at the time, so hotdogs and hamburgers were our standard dinner entrees."

As she listened to her husband reflect on the attributes of the little apartment where they started their cruise of wedded bliss, Ann chuckled and added, "Leave it to a man. Frank has fond memories of the little porch as a place where he grilled food. My memory of the porch is going out there to hang our laundry on the clothesline that Frank rigged between two chimneys. You see, when Frank rented the apartment the thought of how and where I would do our laundry never crossed his mind. The house did not have a laundry room and our financial means didn't permit going to a Laundromat or professional laundry. Therefore, I washed our clothes in the sink, wrung them out by hand and then hung them out to dry on a pulley operated clothesline that my handy husband rigged between two chimneys on the roof, which I could access from the little porch. The clothes dried fine, but usually came off the line dirtier than when I hung them out because of soot from the chimneys. Of course, considering the era, that was a rather insignificant problem and in truth, we shared some very happy times in that little apartment. Sadly, the house is now gone and a business now stands in its place."

Ann's bit of nostalgia inspired a tribute to her and to marriage, spoken in the context and words of a sea captain. "During 50years Ann and I have faced many challenges much more daunting than the problem of doing laundry. We have sailed upon many dangerous financial waters, challenged hidden reefs and shoals that could easily sink our businesses or ruin our marriage, and often it seemed our ship would flounder but my first-mate never sought to abandon ship. It seemed every challenge and time of difficulty only increased our love and devotion for each other. Many times when I drifted off course and put us in danger of running aground, Ann bolstered my spirit, got us back on course, and we returned to profitable and friendly seas."

The Pabst's sojourn in the 3ʳᵈ floor love nest, without a laundry, would be short-lived, as a few months into their honeymoon they happily learned Ann was expecting their first child. When Frank informed his boss, George Bouyea that he was about to become a father and was looking for a larger home for his family, Bouyea told him that he owned a house at 69 Miller Street in Plattsburgh and would sell it to Frank at a price he could afford.

"George Bouyea was a wonderful man to work for," Frank attests, "and he was just an all around wonderful human being. I bought the house and Ann and I moved our meager possessions into the house that would become our home for the next 50 years. It was not an elegant home by any means, but it was comfortable and large enough to accommodate a growing family. It would also serve as refuge from the rigors and stress encountered throughout many years of operating businesses that could be making money one month and losing money the next.

"After moving into our first real home," Frank relates, "Ann and I were quite happy and snug. Now that we owned our own home, the only thing missing was children and we managed to solve that issue in quick order. Eric, our first-born - a handsome little fellow who naturally resembled his dad - was born in 1957. Jaime arrived in 1959. Our first daughter Tracy was born in 1960, followed by Shari in 1961. They were all handsome, beautiful kids and Ann and I felt truly blessed. Shortly after her birth, Shari was diagnosed as having a mild heart problem, which – as we were told – should not prevent her from leading a normal, happy life." Frank's blue eyes began to tear up as he continued and he removed a handkerchief to dry them as he related, "When Shari was two years old, I was on a diving trip down to Lake George and I received an unexpected telephone call from Ann. Ann told me that I needed to return home as Shari was ill and not doing well. We took her to a pediatrician who issued a prescription that would supposedly help her. However, Shari's condition grew progressively worse. We called the pediatrician and he issued a stronger prescription. The medication did not seem to help her. We rushed her to the hospital, where she underwent emergency heart surgery. The surgery was successful, but she had weakened from illness and we lost her. It was the most horrible time in our lives. I think that only someone who has lost a child can relate to the extreme sadness and depression that we felt. Thank God that my wife came from such strong stock. Although feeling as if her heart had been torn from her body, Ann realized that she still had three children to nurture and so she suffered stoically through this tragic time in our lives. We decided that perhaps a way of recovering was to bring another child into our lives, so we started working with an adoption agency and adopted a beautiful little girl whom we named Jody. Ann and I were blessed with kids who loved and respected their parents, although I must admit that their mother deserves recognition for raising them right. As you can imagine, I was always very busy trying to make the money necessary to pay the bills and didn't devote as much time as I should have with my children. Our children are now successful adults and we are quite proud of them. Eric sort of followed in my footsteps, having great affection for Lake Champlain, a wonderful knowledge of boats and enjoys life in the North Country. He is a Harbor Master on Lake Champlain in the summer months and manages the Bear town Ski Center in the winter months. He is still a bachelor. Jim is a well-known, successful surveyor in Detroit, Michigan. He is married to a lovely girl and they have two beautiful children – grandchildren that we, of course, love dearly. Tracy is a social worker and has worked in Nebraska, Alaska and Washington. She married an Air Force pilot who is now a commercial pilot flying Boeing 747's for a major airline. They have a beautiful home near Tacoma Washington. Jody graduated from Vassar College, then, graduated from law school in Massachusetts, where she met Michael, who would become her husband. Jody is presently working for a law firm in Chicago, Illinois and is senior counsel representing Walgreens. Jody and Michael (also an attorney) presented us with two handsome and delightful grandchildren, Kayla and Max. Needless to say, I am proud of all my children and shake my head in amazement when I realize that they make more in a day that I made in a year."

Underwater Adventures

Although working at several jobs, Frank could not resist the lure of the lake and constantly dreamed of the day when he could operate his own business that would be associated with the lake and that would provide a substantial income to support his family.

Before getting married and while living in Elizabethtown, Frank befriended some fellows who shared his interest in underwater diving and this mutual interest would result in some interesting experiences.

Frank displays a warm smile and chuckles often as he relates, "Stubb Longware, Jack Farrell, Hector Sandburg, Roy Holt and Ralph Fillion are great guys, who like me, worked hard and partied hard. We hit it off and shared some real nice times together on and around Lake Champlain. We started diving around 1957 and, as you can imagine, we didn't have a lot of money and our diving gear was antiquated. But we were like steel and the lake was like a magnet. We were drawn to Lake Champlain and focused our diving on shipwrecks that would provide artifacts. We befriended a pilot by the name of Harold Sisko who lived in Port Kent and although he wasn't a diver, he became part of our cadre. On a clear day, Harold would fly over islands and shallows in the lake and chart anomalies in the water, which we would subsequently dive on. One of our first and most interesting dives was in Westport on the sight where the famous lake steamer *Champlain* sank in 1875. The *Champlain II* was quite a vessel in its day. It measured 258' x 35' and carried passengers to and from every port on the lake. Late one evening in 1875, shortly after leaving Westport and under the control of an officer flying high on narcotics, the *Champlain* struck a rock ledge at Rock Harbor, which is just north of the entrance to Westport Bay. The ship started taking on water and sank; however, as

31

it was close to shore, everyone aboard was rescued. As the vessel sank, it broke in half and the aft portion remained on the ledge at a depth of around 10 feet. The bow slid down the cliff face and was at a depth of around 160 feet. Stubb, Jack, and I dove on the wreck and decided to salvage the rudder. We spent several weekends on that wreck site using a hacksaw to cut the bronze pintels and gudgeon's that secured the rudder to the hull. Each pintel and gudgeon weighed about 100 pounds and the rudder was massive measuring 7 ½' x 8'. After several weekends of sawing, we managed to cut the rudder off the boat. We laid it alongside the wreckage on the ledge for later retrieval because we needed better equipment to raise the rudder and bring it in to shore. The boat we used as our dive platform consisted of a couple of inner tubes attached to 2 x 4's. It more resembled a raft than a boat and the only reason it could be called a boat was because we had attached a 4 horsepower motor to it. Although it didn't look too seaworthy, our homemade boat was neat for diving because we had a hatch cut in the center that permitted a diver and his equipment easy access and exit from the water without tipping the boat. Although suitable for diving, the motorized platform wasn't rigged to lift the heavy rudder and haul it in to shore. The fourth Sunday, we borrowed a small salvage boat and went out to retrieve our prize rudder, but it was gone! We had put in many hours and worked very hard to cut the rudder free and needless to say, we were quite angry that someone – who obviously had been watching our labor – stole it. We made some inquiries and learned that Jim Morse, who owned the Essex Marina, had the rudder. He had been monitoring our labor on the Champlain wreck site and knew we wouldn't be able to bring the rudder in with our little homemade diving boat. He went down to the Champlain wreck site in his work barge that had a small crane, lifted the rudder and took it to his marina. He mounted the *Champlain* rudder on a pedestal at the entrance to the restaurant at his marina, which was appropriately named *The Rudder Club* and used it as advertising. To the best of my knowledge, the rudder is still housed in that restaurant at Essex. This episode did not endear Jimmy Morse to us, but I am a believer in the adage 'what goes around, comes around and I figured that one day I would get even and, although it took a few years, I did. It came to pass that a contractor from Willsboro came to me and related that Jimmy Morse had placed a bid with the telephone company to put three miles of cable in the lake, down at Willsboro. At the time I owned the Juniper and Jimmy had a small barge with a crane on it. This contractor friend of mine was miffed at Jimmy because he had put in a bid for the job and Jimmy underbid him by $500. I told him to wait until five minutes before the telephone company closed out acceptance of bids and put in a bid that was $500 less than Jimmy Morse's. My contractor friend was skeptical as to whether the job would turn a profit and I assured him that it would. He did as I told him and won the job. The telephone company planned on it taking two weeks to lay the three miles of cable down. I brought the Juniper down to Willsboro and we completed the job in 18 hours. We worked out of Willsboro Bay Marina, currently owned by Bob Kline, but at that time, it was owned by Ad Derbyshire. The marina had an old crane with a Murphy diesel engine that had about an 80foot boom, and the crane was going to serve as our staging area. The maneuverability of the Juniper was unbelievable. It was 65 feet long and I was turning it around in an area with only 85 feet of clearance. The telephone company was amazed at how fast we completed the job and they flew an engineer up to see how we were able to do it so fast. The engineer told me that the company had based their speed at laying cable on their company cable laying barge *Cable Queen,* which was down in Queens."

The engineer asked, "How did you manage to lay three miles of underwater cable in just 18 hours?"

I responded, "you were paying me by the job. If you were paying by the hour, it would have taken me two weeks. As it turned out, I made a good chunk of money on that job and earned the satisfaction of beating Jimmy Morse out of the money."

Interestingly, what happened to divers diving on the *Champlain* wreck site would inspire Frank and his diving buddies to start a dive club. Frank relates, "Two young lads – as I recall – around 12 – 13 years old purchased some scuba gear. Back in those days you could buy all sort of equipment but not all of it was suitable for deep water diving. Some equipment had airplane regulators that had been converted for diving purposes. If a diver went too deep with them they'd implode. Anyway, these two lads decided to dive on the wreck of the *Champlain* and they likely had defective equipment and certainly minimal instruction about diving. When the *Champlain* sunk, the vessel broke in half. The front of the ship slid down the underwater face of the mountain and settled to the bottom in very deep water. When we dove on the wreck, we discovered that right off the end of mid-ship the mountainside sloped at about a sixty-degree angle. When they dove, the two kids apparently went over the deep drop and down the cliff face. One made it back to the surface, the other one didn't. We - Stubb, Jack and myself - were contacted by the authorities investigating the kid's drowning and asked if we could go down to look for the lost diver. It was believed that he was on the bottom about 160 feet down and we didn't have the equipment to make a deep-water dive. None of us would make the dive unless we had a decompression chamber immediately available. So they obtained the service of a professional diver from the Troy-Albany area. This guy came up with sets of double tanks and he looked like he had the right equipment and knew what he was doing. On his first dive, he didn't find the drowning victim and returned to the surface. He smoked a cigarette, downed a beer, then put on the second set of double tanks and went down again. Again, he was unable to locate the victim and returned to the surface. He smoked another cigarette, drank another beer, strapped on a 3rd set of doubles and went down again. He did not come back up and they never found his body either. That incident caused us to create a diving club for the purpose of educating inspiring divers and teaching them diving safety. We invited young people who were interested in the underwater world to come with us and we taught them snorkeling and basic diving procedures with an emphasis on safety. Eventually the YMCA started a similar program, but their program was connected to a physical fitness course. My philosophy has always been that if you take a guy who's out of shape and drinking a six-pack per day, and turn him into a perfect physical specimen, he will start to believe he can leap tall buildings in a single bound. The first time he gets into a jam, he's going to take a physical approach to resolve the problem rather than using his brain to think his way out of the problem. That's the guy who winds up on the bottom, out of air and out of life. The guy who stops, thinks and gets control of the situation is the one who survives. I would point out that panic is what kills most divers. The original name for our dive club was quite sophisticated. We dubbed ourselves *"The Lake Champlain Underwater Research Club."* After a few beers no one could say our name straight so we shortened our club name to *'Wreck Raiders.'* Essentially that's what it was. We focused our diving jaunts on the site of sunken shipwrecks. When we went diving we had work gloves on, we had crowbars, hammers and we were sacking and pillaging. We recovered a lot of historic relics and we weren't the only crew hunting for treasure. This led to a public outcry and in the early 70's New York and Vermont passed legislation forbidding the removal of artifacts from beneath the surface of the lake. Some folks may find it hard to believe, but I believe this is good legislation, because too many historic items were being scavenged for profit and were sold into private collections, depriving the public from seeing and enjoying their history. Of course one has to remember that in order to interest people in what is down there you've got to bring some of it up. But when historic items are brought up, I believe they belong in a museum where they can be seen and enjoyed by everyone. Leaving everything on the bottom is not logical. But when elected state representatives started listening to howls from environmentalists, it was only a matter of time until laws were passed to restrict what divers were allowed to bring up from the lake and restrictions on what could be done with the items permissible to bring up."

The passage of legislation - endorsed by both New York and Vermont – restricting lake salvage, did not deter the *Wreck Raiders* from diving on wreck sites and exploring them.

Frank explains, "We were really into providing training and instruction to folks who had an interest and zeal for underwater diving and we were about the only act around in the North Country, during the early sixties that provided this training. Much of our training focused on safe diving procedures because we wanted divers to enjoy their underwater adventures but always return to the surface. Naturally, in the process I was always searching for ways to make a few bucks, so I opened up a dive shop located in the marina at Valcour. I named this business *Sub Aqua* and it was quite successful for a number of years. I think it would be fair to say that throughout the sixties *Sub Aqua* was one of the leading dive shops in upstate New York. Of course, being an adventurer and business entrepreneur, I couldn't stay focused on just running a dive shop. When I started up the *Juniper,* the dive shop was sold and it eventually fell by the wayside. The scuba shop led to many adventures, one of them – probably the most outstanding – was the discovery of Mabel Smith Douglas in the waters of Lake Placid." (This adventure occupies its own chapter).

Another quite famous dive, which also occupies its own chapter, resulted in the recovery of two cannons from the lake bottom in Cliff Haven. Frank did not participate in this dive, but club members did, and Frank's salvage barge was used to lift the cannons from the bottom and bring them in to shore.

Although the *Lake Champlain Underwater Research Club*, later shortened to *Wreck Raiders,* **was formed for exploration of ship wrecks and training, club members - because of their skill and ability to stay underwater - started to be called upon for the gruesome task of searching for drowning victims. One instance, in 1967, well documented in the** *Plattsburgh Press-Republican***, involved the search for a 12year old drowning victim in Cumberland Bay. The article begins: "Scuba divers this morning were to begin the second full day of searching for a 12year old boy believed drowned in Cumberland Bay Saturday afternoon. This morning's operations was to start near a marker buoy set late Sunday at the spot where divers brought the windshield of a boat from the water. The windshield was believed to be from the 14foot fiberglass boat Airman 1ˢᵗ Class Dewayne Adamson of 5534E Montana Drive and his 12year old son James had been in before it capsized about 130yards off the western shore of Cumberland Head Saturday afternoon. Adamson was rescued after nearly two hours in the chill waters, but no trace of the boy was found although State Police, firemen and civilian and Air Force volunteers joined the search...Aiding in the search were Civil Air Patrol and U.S. Coast Guard planes; members of the** *"Wreck Raiders"* **Diving Club, under the supervision of the Clinton County Sheriff's Department...High waves estimated at 3 ½ to 4 ½ feet may have been responsible for capsizing the boat...Frank Pabst,** *"Wreck Raiders"* **diver, emerging after a chilly session on an underwater sled said "it's like trying to see through a bunch of feathers down there..."**

Frank recalls, "The small boat capsized just off Cumberland Point in very rough water. The water temperature was only 45 degrees, which contributed to the drowning. Unexpectedly being thrown into the water would have caused immediate shock and hypothermia would set in very quickly. It was sort of miraculous that the boy's father was saved and he was in rough shape when he was pulled from the water by another boater. Very poor underwater visibility greatly hampered our search for the kid. I don't think his body was found and it was very sad."

Frank is quick to tell anyone that the era of the *Wreck Raiders* was a very happy time for him. "It was a great group of guys and we got together on weekends, did training exercises, dove on shipwrecks, thrilled at salvaging artifacts, drank beer and shared a lot of laughs. Although some people – unfamiliar with what we did – accused the *Wreck Raiders* of being scavengers, we really were not. One of our main interests was preserving history. We placed most of the stuff we brought up from our dives - grape shot, pieces of ship armament, pieces of uniform, muskets, sabers, etc. - in a building behind my house and petitioned the City of Plattsburgh to create a museum there so people could come view the pieces of history and enjoy them."

A small blurb in the sports section of the *Plattsburgh Press-Republican* in 1963, attests to Frank's attempts to establish the museum: "Lake Champlain Underwater Research Club led by Frank Pabst and Roy Holt push for museum at 75 Miller Street to commemorate naval battles on Lake Champlain." Another blurb in the same sports section reported: "Randall Larkin, Dick Niffenegger, Tom Kaiser, Jack Fitzpatrick and Frank Pabst reach 155 feet in a bounce dive."

Frank attests, "Over the years I had both positive and negative dealings with City government, depending on the Mayor and administration in power. Unfortunately, my plans for a museum never came to fruition because those in power at the time were opposed and eventually we gave up on the idea."

The lead paragraph in an editorial appearing in the *Plattsburgh Press-Republican* on April 18, 2003, made reference to the museum proposed by Pabst. It begins: "It was just a small note in the Press-Republican's "The Week in Sports," which ran in Monday's edition. Under "40years ago (in 1963)," it said, "The Lake Champlain Underwater Research Club, led by …That museum never came to pass. Like many ventures in which Pabst was to align himself over the next four decades, its potential was never realized…""

"I think the public, especially school kids," Frank explains in slight note of sadness, "would have enjoyed their visit to a museum totally focused on the history of Lake Champlain and they would have taken away knowledge and a new sense of appreciation for the lake."

Of course the museum failure did not deter the *Wreck Raiders* and they continued exploring the lake at every opportunity

In reflection on some of their more notable diving experiences, Frank recalls, "Contrary to what many folks believe, we were dedicated to preserving history and concerned about the environment of the lake. We never made much money from any of the stuff we brought up and mostly turned everything over to museums and historical societies. For example, we were diving out by *Crab Island* and found bronze plaques that vandals had removed from the monument on the island that pays tribute to the American and British dead that were buried on the island in 1814. We turned those plaques over to the Plattsburgh Air Force Base Museum. We were diving near the entrance to the Salmon River, down in Valcour, and found a turbine that had been used by a mill at the mouth of the river circa 1900. We turned the homemade turbine over to the Kent-DeLord House (home seized by the British and used as their headquarters during their siege of Plattsburgh in 1814 – turned into a museum), and unfortunately, the folks at Kent-Delord decided it didn't have any value and burned it. Sadly, they destroyed a piece of history. This turbine was an unusual device. It was a log about 20feet long and had square oak pegs driven in one end that would drive a square link chain. It had 3-foot oak fins angled at one end and which resembled propellers. I figured out how the turbine worked and it was quite ingenious. The log was set in the end of a sluice and when water hit it, it would spin and generate energy to power the mill and blast furnace. As naval battles were fought in the area of Valcour Island during both the Revolutionary War and War of 1812, there were a lot of shipwrecks and a lot of ordnance lying on the bottom in that area. When we first started diving around Valcour, we went down wearing just mask and snorkel and filled pails with cannon grape shot in about fifteen minutes. We took all the treasure we hauled up from the bottom to our museum on Miller Street. Our museum was a vacant, former schoolhouse just two doors from my residence. The city leased the building to me for $1 year. That building was the *Wreck Raiders* clubhouse and maritime museum. We brought the artifacts recovered from the lake to the museum and drink a few beers while we organized and set up displays. We had a number of great things on display: For example, we had canister shot that still had the canvas on which Ralph Fillion donated; Hector Sandburg donated anchors that went back to the 1600's; we had a cannon that Dave Hall brought in and it weighed about 1200 pounds; we had muskets, cannonballs, shot and a lot of other items – all on display. Schools would come in and half the class would go to the Kent-DeLord house, during one part of the day, while the other half would come to our museum, then they'd switch around for the other part of the day. Our museum was doing quite well until somebody in City government got a bug up their rear end. The city administration voted not to renew my lease on the building and forced us to close the museum. It was a shame because our operation had been approved by the New York State Education Department and children were making field trips to our museum from schools located all over the North Country. This was actually the first museum totally dedicated to Lake Champlain underwater history and it was responsible for me becoming acquainted with Hollywood movie star Buster Crabbe." (This reflection caused Frank to digress and relate memories of his relationship with the famous movie star of the 1940-50's era.) "He was a real strong and handsome man, had a great personality and was just an all around nice person."

For those readers unfamiliar with the late Buster Crabbe - he was an excellent swimmer, who won a bronze medal for swimming in the 1928 Olympics and a gold medal for swimming in the 1932 Olympics. He became a Hollywood movie star, appearing in several movies as *Tarzan*. He also portrayed Flash Gordon and Buck Rogers in early Science Fiction films, had the lead role in several western films and portrayed *Captain Gallant of the Foreign Legion* on television. In the mid 1950's, Crabbe purchased a defunct prep school located in Onchiota New York, which was near Plattsburgh, named it the Buster Crabbe Meenahga Lodge and opened it as a swimming camp for children between the ages of 8-14 (Wikipedia).

Frank continued, "Buster was fascinated by the beauty and history of Lake Champlain and he brought some students over to our museum in Plattsburgh. Naturally, I enthralled them with stories about the lake's history and the role it played in shaping America. I guess my blarney enthralled Buster too, because he purchased some diving equipment from me and we became friends. I took him out on the lake for a dive and he enjoyed the experience so much that he discussed going into business with me to operate a chain of dive shops throughout the United States. To my chagrin, that vision never progressed beyond the planning stages and Buster went into the swimming pool business instead. Buster was not the stereotypical image of most movie heroes. He was a principled man who stayed married to the same woman throughout life. He was a widower when I met him because his wife had died in 1959. I guess they had a couple of kids but I never met them and don't know much about them. Buster passed away in 1983 and his death made me very sad. Buster introduced me to Lloyd Bridges, who at the time was famous for his television show *Sea Hunt*." I loved the show so much I used the name *Sea Hunt* as logo for my sub-aqua dive shop. Buster introduced Lloyd to me because Lloyd was looking for some underwater artifacts that he could use in a display at the 1964 World's Fair, which was going to be in New York City. He told me that he wanted to put the artifacts in a tank of water where Bridges was going to pretend to wrestle an octopus. He told me that if I donated the artifacts, he would put a display board outside the tank identifying the artifacts as recovered from Lake Champlain in Plattsburgh, New York. I thought it was a great idea that would entice tourists to this area. The only problem was, the cost involved to get the items down to New York and positioned in the tank was $125 and, at the time, I didn't have two nickels to rub together. I asked the City of Plattsburgh if they would spend the $125 for the value of attracting tourists and was turned down. I was told that the city was paying for a band from Peru to go to the World's Fair and therefore they couldn't afford it. This was one of my first tender experiences with the short sightedness of government. I couldn't get the money, so the artifacts didn't appear in the World's Fair and Plattsburgh lost the opportunity for some real cheap advertising for tourism."

Like Buster Crabbe, Lloyd Bridges was a famous 1940-1970 stage, movie and television star. He appeared in over 100 movies and 32 television productions. He passed away in 1998 at the age of 85. (Wikipedia)

Story about Buster Crabbe and Lloyd Bridges told, Frank returned to his reflection on the fate of the *Wreck Raiders* museum, displaying a trace of anger on his normally jovial face. "All of the treasure we had in our museum was taken over to the Kent-DeLord house. For some idiotic reason known only to the directors of Kent-DeLord, they destroyed many of the artifacts. It was a shame, because items that were important pieces of Lake Champlain history were destroyed."

In 1960, Frank opened his sub-aqua dive shop at the Valcour Marina. His reflection: "My first dive shop was in a dog kennel located in the back of Bill's Sport Shop at the Valcour Marina. I decided to open up a dive shop because the guy who was selling diving equipment in town was selling it at a multiple sport shop. So diving was just another wart on the cucumber of diving. (Ingenious how these euphemisms so easily spill from the Captain) I say my shop was in a dog kennel because Bill was into dogs and he had a dog kennel in back of the dive shop. My original dive shop was in the building that presently serves as the office for Snug Harbor and Valcour Marina. After a short time, I moved the dive shop across Route 9 and into what had been a pump house for the D & H railroad. The building needed a lot of repair. I fixed the roof of the building and then had to address the filling of trenches in the floor, which had been placed there to accommodate water pipes. There was also a 16" hole in the back wall of the building. Then, there was a sump pit with intake lines coming in from the lake, the purpose of which is sort of interesting to railroad history buffs. Back in the days of steam engines, water was pumped out of the lake and into the pit. The water was then pumped from the pit to the south rail yard in Plattsburgh. Trains coming in with steam engines would fill up their boilers with water, while they were discharging passengers. It was a real good system. Pumps and the motors that powered them were bolted to big concrete blocks on the side of the pit that was about 16 feet deep and 4 feet square in the center of the floor. There were a couple of 16inch square trenches in the floor as well, with another trench going out the back of the building; this trench contained the discharge line. Water was continually pumped in from the lake and then pumped out to the railroad yard. When the steam locomotive faded into obscurity, the pump house was closed down and with the passage of years, fell into disrepair. Because of the pits in the floor and the building needing a lot of work, I was able to get it for a song and you can imagine how cheap that was because I can't carry a tune. Of course, in order to use the building for a dive shop I needed to fix it up and fill the holes in the floor with concrete. This presented a slight dilemma because I didn't have the money to purchase the concrete. One of our divers in the *Wreck Raiders* happened to be an inspector for the government and I knew there was a lot of concrete work being done at Plattsburgh Air Force Base at the time. I asked him if he ever rejected a load of concrete that was going into a government project. He told me that he had and, as a matter of fact, there would be a load rejected and brought down to my place for pouring at around three-thirty in the afternoon on a specific day in the following week. With the help of five or six dive club members we repaired the roof and got ready for the concrete delivery. That day I purchased five or six cases of beer and the guys showed up with rakes and shovels. Needless to say, we had consumed a lot of beer by the time the cement truck arrived, so we were ready to tackle the job with enthusiasm. A chute was positioned to have the concrete flow into the hole that we wanted to fill. When everything was positioned, the cement truck driver started releasing his load. My work crew and myself were standing by the 16 inch hole in the back of the building waiting for the concrete to come down a chute and through the hole. The concrete started coming in and we were attacking it with a vengeance, but it was coming in frustratingly slow. So I hollered out to the concrete truck driver, 'is that as fast as that stuff runs?"

The driver yelled back, "No, I can give it to you faster."

"Within 20 seconds we were knee deep in concrete. It was amazing how fast the concrete poured in. It came in like a huge cow evacuating her intestines. It was a huge mess. Anyway, with a lot of labor, we got the holes in the floor fixed and four inches of concrete into the pit and then we built a lid to cover the remainder of the hole. Thanks to dedicated club members, who loved drinking beer and sharing a good time together, I got the shop up and running for the price of a few beers. The dive shop didn't make enough money to support my growing family; however, I still was driving truck for Bouyea Bakery at the time and considered the dive shop as a business write off. Of course, getting burglarized a couple of times detracted from profitability and really pissed me off. Interestingly, my cash register was located in a position near the cover over the pit. After the second break-in, I removed the pit cover when I closed up and replaced it with some pieces of lath that would break if someone stepped on them. I also mounted some fish spears down in the pit to ensure anyone foolish enough to burgle me again wouldn't get away. The fire department somehow got wind of my burglar trap and informed me to eliminate the trap, as I was setting myself up for either criminal or civil liability. My experience of being the victim of an attempted robbery while driving a taxi left me with a permanent hatred of thieves and somehow, it doesn't seem logical that a businessman or home owner should be held responsible for injuring or even killing someone who breaks into his premises to steal." Having made this statement, Frank chuckles and adds, "Actually, what happened at another one of my businesses sort of proved that the fire chief had given me good advice."

Displaying a sheepish grin, Frank continued to chuckle as he reflected on that incident.

"Around 1964, I had the opportunity to open up another dive shop over in Burlington. It was located at the old salt dock there, and, in order to get the place, I had to remove pilings from the old salt dock. I figured the quickest and easiest way to get rid of them was by blasting them out. I bought some RDX explosives, some primer cord and blasting caps. As it turned out, all I needed was the primer cord because the blast of prima cord would shoot the pilings off real neat. So I had the RDX left over and I put that into a fridge that we had in the dive shop. One day a thunderstorm came up and a bolt of lightning hit a wire that I had rigged up for dive shop lighting. The energy from that lightning bolt entered the building, and blew two guys that were in the building right across the room. Fortunately, it didn't set off the RDX or the blasting caps. Those guys would have been seriously injured, perhaps even killed and if that had happened, I would have faced either criminal or civil liability, or perhaps both."

The *Sub Aqua* dive shop became a new focal point for the *Wreck Raiders* and as it was located at Valcour, it was quite near the channel where the club dove on numerous shipwrecks. "During the life of my sub aqua shop, we had some great times," Frank attests. "Of course, diving is an expensive pastime, because in addition to diving equipment, divers need a boat to operate from. As I didn't have much money and lacked established credit, the word 'new' was not in my vocabulary. I scrounged around and found a well-used boat for sale up in Lake Placid. Although I refer to it as my boat, it actually belonged to the entire dive club. It was a 32foot, outboard, Consolidated boat, made out of dark mahogany. We brought the boat up to Plattsburgh, named her the *Sea Witch* and painted her black. We put a big Homelite outboard motor on it and this became my first dive boat. I kept the *Sea Witch* for 5 or 6 years and although nothing to look at, she served us well."

Reflection on the tenure of the *Sea Witch* produces another anecdote from the Captain.

"One day, I took a group of people up to Chambly, Canada on the *Sea Witch*. They were folks who belonged to the Plattsburgh Yacht Club, which was out of my league. Anyway, we started partying on the boat and we were anchored up on the Chambly. I didn't have any drinking glasses on board, but I did have a small saucepan. I poured the pan half full of whiskey, the other half with 7up and passed it around like a peace pipe. No one seemed to mind and it was probably because they were all inebriated. Doctor Dave Weeks was sitting there smoking one of his ubiquitous cigars and he asked me what he should do with the ashes. I told him, "You're standing on the ashtray." Those folks were all used to partying on fancy yachts, and the *Sea Witch* was just a good workboat."

Captain Frank Pabst and his *Wreck Raiders* charted and dove on many shipwrecks, most of which were in Lake Champlain; but they also explored the depths of lakes and rivers in other areas of New York State, other states and even Canada. Although the club was formed for the purpose of training divers and engaging in recreation diving, their ability to conduct deep water dives resulted in frequent requests from authorities to conduct searches for drowning victims. Expertise both above and below the water led to Frank being named by Clinton County Sheriff Paul 'Chick' Guay – in 1966 - to head the Clinton County Sheriff's Department underwater search and rescue team.

"At the time," Frank recalls, "the method used by most police departments to recover bodies from water was by dragging a metal bar containing 50-60 large fish hooks, connected to rope or chain, on the bottom. If and when the body was hooked, it was brought up like a prize show fish and the hooks caused considerable damage to the body. (The author can attest to this, as in 1963, while a young trooper in the New York State Police, he and Trooper Marvin Cole recovered the body of a young drowning victim in Oneida Lake, using a drag. It was not a pleasant experience) Frank continues: "The *Wreck Raiders* became noted for our ability to dive deep and recover drowning victims, and this led to my forming one of the first underwater search and recovery teams in New York State. As our reputation spread, we were called upon to search for drowning victims and victims of homicide in many jurisdictions."

Eventually, Sheriff Guay asked Frank to also take charge of the Clinton County Marine Patrol on Lake Champlain.

"Paul was a good friend of mine," Frank attests, "and I ran the marine patrol for 7 years for the Sheriff's department. During that time, I owned the boats that were used for patrol and leased them to the Sheriff's Department. My divers were provided law enforcement training and there was a lot of enforcement needed on the lake at that time. Toward the end of our tenure things started getting more serious. Guys with Donzi's and cigarette boats would blast across the Canadian border carrying loads of illicit drugs and we were requested to try and stop them. As my marine patrol did not carry firearms at the time, I thought the request was unreasonable. I told the Sheriff, "If you want us to stop boats like that you had better arm us with shotguns, because I'm not going to try to apprehend dangerous guys like that with peashooters.""

Returning reflection to various notable dives by the *Wreck Raiders* Frank relates, "We were called and asked to go up to Canandaigua Lake to search for the body of a woman who was the victim of a homicide. As I recall, we were informed that the owner of a store conveyor company had garroted his wife, then, set her on fire using ether or starter fluid. After trying to destroy her identity, he stuffed her in a weighted barrel and dumped the barrel into water that was about 150 feet deep. Gary Brandstetter, Dan Hobbs, Donny McGowan and myself went up to join in the deepwater search. We arrived up there in the late afternoon and were put up in rooms at a Holiday Inn. The authorities had called a lot of dive teams to participate in the search because the water was so deep that divers were burned out quickly. The following morning we were preparing to dive and were informed that a United States Navy dive team, who had preceded us and were using sonar, had located the barrel. It was an interesting experience. We were also called up to Rackett Lake to search for a person who had been missing for about two weeks and was presumed to have drowned. We found the body by the quantity of Catfish (Bullheads) that swirled around it. Only about a third of the body was recoverable, because the fish had eaten the rest of it."

The main focus of the *Wreck Raiders* would continue to be exploring shipwrecks and those adventures alone would create a thick book. For the purpose of his biography, Frank reflected on some of the most memorable experiences.

"I had read an account published by Oscar Bredenburg," Frank recalls, "in which he reports that one of General Benedict Arnold's gunboats had sunk over on the east side of the lake in Arnold's Bay. Supposedly, the boat was located in shallow water just off the end of a reef, which was marked by a huge rock near where a small stream entered the southeast corner of the bay. Using these directions, we dove off the end of the reef but the water had the viscosity of pea soup and I had virtually no underwater visibility. I swam around with my arms outstretched and all of a sudden I was straddle one of the ribs of Arnold's boat and I smacked my head into it. We were delighted to have found the historic vessel and we mucked around on the bottom for quite some time. We were excited when we found some grape shot and a human wrist bone. Upon completing our dive, we went into shore and rested near the big rock and popped open a six-pack of beer to wet our whistle. As we sat there enjoying our beer we suddenly realized that if we had started our search from the shore, rather than the lake, we could have walked right to the shipwreck. That incident wasn't written up in any newspapers.

The owners of Ausable Chasm started up a display that they referred to as a museum. Payson Hatch, John Keel and Walt or Joe Church had an extensive collection of old cars on display there and they added three boats that were recovered from the lake. As I recall, one of the boats was the steamer *Vermont,* which was the first successful commercial steamboat on Lake Champlain. The other two boats were displayed as General Benedict Arnold's gunboats, which were nothing but ribs and planks. Before Arnold's gunboats were brought up from the lake, we dove on their location several times and salvaged some artifacts from the Revolutionary War era. One of my dive buddy's was well-known North Country radio and television personality, Gordie Little, and he made a dive with me on the Arnold gunboats. We found some grapeshot on that dive and Gordie was quite excited about the experience. Gordie and I became good friends and over the years I was a guest several times on his radio show. He videotaped some sessions with me, related to diving, the Juniper, lake salvage and other issues, and these interviews were programmed on the local television station. Anyway, the boats that were on display at Ausable were not well preserved. They were kept in an open shed where they were exposed to the elements and they deteriorated rapidly. In the late 70's the owners of the Ausable Chasm operation decided to start operating a campsite. When I learned of this, I wondered what they intended to do with the boats because they were such rare historical finds. I had discussed the need to protect and preserve the boats with the Ausable Chasm owners and they had assured me they would be protected. I went down to Ausable to inquire about acquiring the boats or having them transferred to another museum and was dismayed to learn that the boats had been buried in the ground by a bulldozer. It seemed a sacrilege, because those boats had played an important role in the shaping of Lake Champlain history. However, in that era the rotting hulks of old boats – despite their history – didn't seem important enough to stand in the way of business expansion or development."

Frank is proud of having founded the *Wreck Raiders* and it was a very enjoyable time in his life, though juggling his schedule to find time to spend driving truck, operating a dive shop, training divers and being involved in lake salvage left him little time to spend with his young family.

"As the *Wreck Raiders* notoriety grew," Frank relates, "we were called upon to travel extensively to conduct searches and recoveries." Face glowing with pride, he continued, "Divers that I trained traveled all over the world to dive and some started making a good living at it. For example, some of my divers went over to the North Sea and conducted deepwater dives for the construction of offshore oil wells. Divers that I had worked with over the years dove on the site of the famous *Andrea Doria*. They had heard that the Italian government was interested in recovering the statue of Admiral Doria, which was in the grand ballroom when the vessel sank. They got a fix on the boat, affixed a line to it, blasted a hole in it, then went inside and recovered the solid bronze statue, which was about 8 feet tall and weighed in the neighborhood of 2000 pounds. I was told they wrapped primer cord around both ankles of the statute, set off the primer cord and then used a shipboard crane to bring the statute to the surface. After recovering the statue, they wired the Italian Consulate and informed them that they had the statue and would exchange it with the Italian government for $250,000. The Italians responded that they were not interested, so they sold the statue to some guy in Florida and the statue wound up as a display in front of a hotel.

We made many dives searching for gold in the vicinity of Valcour and Garden Island. The story of how that gold came to be in the lake has been documented by historians, which leads me to believe it to be true and, although we scoured the bottom many times, we were never able to locate ship wreckage or gold. Many divers have searched and continue to search for the illusive treasure, but to my knowledge, no one has been successful. Of course, if they were successful, knowing that the gold - by law - had to be turned over to the state, its recovery might be a well-kept secret. How the gold ended up in the lake is interesting. In 1751 a French ship came down from Canada with its destination being Fort Carillon located at the south end of the lake. When the British defeated the French and captured the fort it was renamed Ticonderoga. The ship was carrying a cargo of 50,000 gold Louis coins, intended as pay for the soldiers stationed at Fort Carillon. Just south of Garden Island, also known as Gunboat Island - a small island just off the south end of Valcour Island - there is a rock reef which continues for about a half mile south of the island. The French ship struck the reef and sank. The Captain of the ship salvaged what he could from the sinking vessel and proceeded to Garden Island in a longboat. They made several trips with the longboat to the sunken vessel, which did not sink below the lake surface as it was hung up on the shallow reef and brought enough wood and equipment to set up a camp on the island. After salvaging what they could and setting up camp, the Captain and a few crewmen proceeded to Fort Carillon in the longboat, to report the loss of his ship. The remainder of the crew was instructed to stay on Garden Island to watch over the wreck and wait for rescue. As the story was told to me, some of the better swimmers in the crew swam back and forth from island to wreck and removed almost 10,000 gold pieces from the 50,000 on board. A tiny contingent of men stayed on the island over the winter, watching the wreck; however, knowing the harshness of winter in the North Country, that was some feat. It was hoped that after the ice broke up in the spring, a ship would arrive from Fort Carillon and the remainder of the valuable cargo would be salvaged. During the winter, ice encapsulated the boat, permitting those camped on the island to walk to it. However, the chests containing the gold were in the ship's hold, which was underwater, and the icy water prevented the crew from getting to them. So they watched and waited for spring to arrive.

What they did not foresee, nor anticipate, was that with the arrival of the warmth of spring, Lake Champlain rises due to the runoff of melting snow coming into it. When the ice started breaking up, the rising water lifted the wreckage from the reef and it drifted away. After enduring a harsh winter to protect the treasure, the crew watched the remains of their ship being carried away and they could do nothing to stop it. I can imagine the helpless, hopeless feelings they must have experienced, as they watched and realized their sacrifice had been for naught. It was reported that the moving ice carried the vessel north of the island, then, released its clutch on the vessel and it sank beneath the waves. Supposedly, the 40,000 remaining gold Louis were never recovered and this story inspired many divers to search for the missing treasure. I believe the *Wreck Raiders* used up a hundred tanks of air searching for it and as it is in about 120 feet of water, it is a difficult search and divers consume air quickly. Someday, someone's going to find the remains of that wreck and it becomes more likely as new and better equipment is developed for underwater search."

Although not successful in finding the French gold pieces, Frank attests that the *Wreck Raiders* did make a very exciting find of small treasure.

He relates, "During the early years of the club, when we still called ourselves the *Lake Champlain Underwater Research Club*, we were diving off Michael's Reef, located on the northeast corner of *Crab Island* and we found the remains of a schooner on the bottom. Mucking in that wreck, we found 30 silver pieces, which was quite exciting. They were Spanish milled dollars that had been minted between 1770-1774. We sold them to coin collectors, one or two at a time.

The *Wreck Raiders* reputation grew and folks interested in underwater diving and exploration radiated to us. We trained a lot of Air Force members, while they were stationed at Plattsburgh Air Force Base, and when they left they spread the word about Lake Champlain and their diving experiences. I wound up becoming President of the New York State Diver's Association, which had approximately 750 members at the time, and that was a very good time in my life. What was happening to all the artifacts that divers were bringing up from the lake was of great concern to me, as I knew most items having great historical value were being sold and ending up in someone's closet, on someone's fireplace mantel or stored in someone's attic. So while President of the

New York State Divers Association, I started petitioning the State to accredit our museum on Miller Street and make it an official museum. I asked that they pass legislation that would require all artifacts brought up from Lake Champlain to become the property of the State and have them put on display in museums, so that everyone could enjoy them. There already was existing legislation under the New York State Education Law, but as I would learn subsequent to our recovery of the Cliff Haven cannons – which the state totally botched – the law was not enforced. (See Chapter – Cannon Recovery @ Cliff Haven). As it turned out, I did not get any cooperation from the City of Plattsburgh and as I previously explained our museum closed."

The *Wreck Raiders* underwater searches for shipwrecks were not always successful and one of the elusive wrecks was the schooner *Nancy*, which despite several dives, was never located.

"I had compiled about four hours of tape recordings relating to the history of shipwrecks on the lake," Frank relates, "and the story of the Schooner *Nancy* so fascinated me, that I was determined to find her remains. There was a lot of fascinating information on those tapes and unfortunately, they were destroyed when my warehouse burned in 1984. From the best of memory, the *Nancy*, a 90foot long canal schooner, commanded by Captain Willy Mock, was hauling a load of coal from Plattsburgh to Burlington and a Ford car dealer cut a deal with Willy to take ten Model T Ford automobiles over to Burlington with his load of coal. Planks were used to load the cars and they were parked on top of the coal. Now Captain Mock was an unusual man. He was only 4' 11" tall and the wheelhouse of his boat was only 5 feet in height. So if you went in there to talk to him, you had to bend over. As it were, Captain Willy overloaded the *Nancy* and the decks were almost awash when he set sail for Burlington. The *Nancy* ran into a squall off of Rock Dunder, at the at the entrance to Burlington Harbor. The overloaded boat was soon swamped and went down just off the point, sinking to the bottom, which was about 120feet down. We spent a lot of time searching for the *Nancy* but at that depth it was difficult to see and we never found her. I can imagine that if found, those Model T Fords would be in pretty decent shape because at that depth they would be preserved. Another of our more interesting dives was on the wreck of the *Phoenix,* which caught fire and sank near Providence Island. We were one of the first dive groups to dive on it and a lot of divers were attracted because it was rumored that there was $8000 in gold and $12000 in silver on board. We found the wreck on the bottom but we didn't find the treasure. The *Phoenix* is now marked on charts as a historic site."

The Sub Aqua dive shop was an enjoyable experience; however, Frank realized that while it required a lot of time, it would never produce the income needed to support his growing family.

"In addition," Frank muttered, "I started having competition from other dive shops. A fellow who was probably drawn to Lake Champlain in much the same fashion as I was, Art Cohn, a lawyer down in New York City came up here in the 60's and started up the *Northern Divers* dive shop in Burlington. I got to know Art and he's aggressive, knows the right people to talk to and is quite successful. Art parlayed his way into becoming Director of the Lake Champlain Maritime Museum, located down in Vergennes and he does a spectacular job with it. He alienated many local divers, but he manages to get permits and gets the job done. I guess he has a lot more finesse than I do when it comes to dealing with politicians. Art and I stayed on friendly terms and I think it is a good thing that the Lake Champlain Maritime Museum came into being. It is a place where people can go and see the wonderful history of the lake. Besides," Frank adds with a sigh, "I had way too many things going on and all of my activities detracted mightily from having quality time with my family. I frequently give thanks to God for allowing me to find and marry the most loving, tolerant and patient woman in the world. When I wasn't working, I was partying and diving with club members, training new divers, salvaging something or involved with the Sheriff's marine patrol. Needless to say, I wasn't spending a lot of time at home, but Ann never harangued me and she did a remarkable job of raising our children. Throughout our now fifty-plus years of marriage, our love for each other never faltered and, when you consider my antics, that is a remarkable achievement. Although there were times Ann surely resented my involvement in so many things, she was also proud of my accomplishments and achievements and, despite some tough financial times, she supported my entrepreneurial ambitions and always had faith that eventually we would enjoy true financial security."

The following two articles, both written by Staff Writer Jeff Meyers, and appearing in the *Plattsburgh Press-Republican*, serve as anecdotal testimony to Frank's feelings about preserving the dignity of Lake Champlain's historical artifacts. The first article appeared in the July 9, 2000 publication under the caption *History Under Water – Lake Champlain Shipwrecks Tell Tales of War, Commerce, Tragedy:* "Ever since humankind has been venturing onto the lakes and oceans of this planet, the world beneath the water's surface has always captured our imaginations. And when sailing vessels are lost, sucked into the depths of those lakes and oceans, our imaginations are amplified by the connection between known and unknown worlds. Famous shipwrecks, like the *Titanic, Edmund Fitzgerald* and Lake Champlain's own *Royal Savage*, have long been the subject of maritime lore and speculation. We yearn to unleash the secrets buried beneath their watery tombs. But Lake Champlain's bottom is a vast graveyard, littered with hundreds of shipwrecks that represent every era of transportation on the lake. Many are still in remarkable shape, protected by the cold, dark water that surrounds them. "There are many things on the lake bottom that represent time capsules of history, from military activities to how early commerce moved," said Frank Pabst, a veteran Lake Champlain diver and captain. "It's history in its purest state," said Pabst, the owner and captain of Juniper Boat Tours. "We see history in museums that's been picked, handled, moved and stored. Here, we see the ships as they are, untouched. That's one of the things that got my passion started on diving." Pabst was diving in Lake Champlain more than 40 years ago when scuba was in its infancy. He often found shipwrecks that hadn't been seen for hundreds of years. "It was quite a thrill," he said. "In those days, everything was pure and unblemished. Now many divers have been on many of these sites. Divers today are interested in preserving wrecks for the next diver, but back then, the basic diving tools were a pair of gloves and a crowbar." What survived the early onslaught of treasure seekers has now become a treasure of its own, the remains of boats and ships that fell prey to the powers of Lake Champlain. "There is a romantic intrigue that surrounds shipwrecks," said Erick Tichonuk from the Lake Champlain Maritime Museum in Basin Harbor, Vt. "*Titanic* is a great example of how shipwrecks capture the human imagination. "Lake Champlain has an incredible collection of just that, and they are so well preserved. We have shipwrecks down there that are 90 percent intact. It's that complete image of what we think a shipwreck is that makes it so romantic." Over the past five seasons, the Maritime Museum has been surveying the lake bottom in search of new and unknown shipwrecks and other artifacts. Each year, the survey vessel covers about 40 square miles of lake bottom, and Tichonuk expects the project to be completed within the next three years. "When we began the survey, we knew approximately 200 shipwrecks had been verified," he said. "Over the course of the past five years, we've found about 50 new wrecks." One of those finds made national headlines when researchers identified the "*Spitfire*," one of the gunboats used by American commander Benedict Arnold during the Battle of Valcour in October 1776. The boat was found upright in deep water, its mast still standing and a canon still mounted on the bow. Researchers now want to decide what would be the best method for saving the boat: leaving it on the lake bottom or bringing it to the surface to preserve and display as a historic relic. The lake-bottom survey was initiated because historians feared that shipwrecks in the lake may be in danger because of the proliferation of zebra mussels. Many wrecks – particularly those in shallow water – have already been encrusted by zebra mussels, though experts don't know what kinds of damage the mollusks may have inflicted on the fragile sunken vessels. "We are in the process to determine what effect it is having on them," Tichonuk said. "They really deserve our protection and respect as they are a perfect window into how humans may have lived. Whether they're military, commercial or recreational, they represent our past. I think very few things can do that as well…"

The second article was published under the caption *Protecting, Sharing Lake Treasures - Public Hears Options on Managing Lake Champlain Wrecks, Artifacts*. "Shipwrecks and other historical artifacts lying on the bottom of Lake Champlain need to be protected, but they also need to be shared with everyone. A few dozen scuba divers and local-history buffs attended a public meeting recently to discuss management options for the lake's archeology treasures.

"We (the public) love shipwrecks," said Art Cohn, executive director of the Lake Champlain Maritime Museum in Basin Harbor, Vt. "In the past, we loved them by raising them (from the lake). There was nothing malicious about their intent, but now we know that raising ships is not good for them." The Maritime Museum, which has actively been mapping the lake bottom over the past five years to identify the location of wrecks and other artifacts, is creating a draft management plan for lake relics. New York State has asked museum officials to develop a plan that includes public interest and future display interests for the artifacts. "The Maritime Museum has no agenda in this," Cohn said. "We want to do a good study and give a good report to quantify any possible future regulations. During the lake-bottom survey, the museum has identified several dozen newly located shipwrecks, about 20 of which would make potential public dive sites," Cohn said. The ideal diving wrecks are in less than 100 feet of water and are not in such sensitive condition that divers might inadvertently cause damage to them. But the states, which have the ultimate authority over the wrecks, will have to decide what direction to take. The public's comments, recorded during the meeting, are an essential part of what might become of the wrecks. *New View:*

"Diving is one of the last frontiers of freedom," said longtime diver and lake salvager Frank Pabst, who felt some kind of record of the location and identity of artifacts is needed for preservation. Like many of the divers on hand, Pabst clearly remembered the time when divers did often remove artifacts and take them home to private collections. But everyone agreed that artifacts were for the public, whether on the lake bottom or on display in area museums.

"I've been diving for 30years, give or take two," said former Plattsburgh Police chief Matt Booth. "I was a hunter and gatherer, as many of us were when we started out. But I've seen a better way of doing things." Booth adamantly believes artifacts should be shared with everyone. "The diving community is rather small," he said. "I would like to bring things back to people who aren't fortunate enough to see them. Our grandchildren need to see how our predecessors lived."

Roger Harwood, a local diver who lives near Valcour Island, feels smaller artifacts should be removed from the lake because he believes people will continue to illegally remove them, and the public will never be able to see them. "There needs to be a mechanism in place where these objects can be taken someplace rather than across the border (to Canada) or to Vermont," he said. "I'm concerned that some of the things out there now are not going to be there."

Steve Nye, a local diver and instructor, said he believes the diving community can play a big role in protecting the artifacts. He also feels opening 20 new dive sites to historic wrecks could greatly improve tourism in the area. (*Place to see artifacts:*) Not all the speakers were divers, however.

Jim Millard, from South Hero, Vt., said he will probably never be able to dive down to shipwrecks, but being an avid lover of local history he relies on divers to help him see what he will never see. "That's why places like the Maritime Museum exist," he said. "We need land-based interpretation (of the sites). You've got to take into account the in-diving public."

Keith Herkalo, the Plattsburgh city clerk and a history buff as well, said, "New technologies such as live video cams can help the public see the shipwrecks that attract so much curiosity."

Several members of the Battle of Plattsburgh Association (Frank was a co-chair of the Association) were on hand as well to lend support to a survey going on in the waters near Valcour Island, where the famous Battle of Valcour took place. They also emphasized the need for a local museum to display the lake's treasures that can and should someday be removed."

Lake Towing & Harbor Salvage

The salvage of a sunken vessel would result in the *Wreck Raiders* traveling to the Caribbean to dive in the waters off the island of St. Croix.

The ruddy sea captain's face glows with excitement as he relates, "It is amazing how my involvement in various aspects of marine work led to so many adventures. For example, when I was operating the *Juniper,* a group of 3 or 4 fellows purchased an old World War II minesweeper and decided to give me competition on the lake." Recollection of the adventure evokes a chuckle from the old sea captain, who continues, "They named their vessel *Mount Independence* and started operation out of Burlington Harbor. One time we challenged each other to a tour boat race and the *Juniper* handily beat the old tub. The *Mount Independence* had a wooden hull which, when making contact with mines, didn't set them off as easily as a steel hull. Anyway, the *Mount Independence* apparently wasn't turning a profit, so they sold the vessel to an individual who tied it up at the water plant in Burlington. The new owner didn't take proper care of the boat and, after riding out several storms at the water plant dock the boat suffered a lot of damage. Canopies fell over the side and a lot of things were broken up. The owner asked me to salvage the vessel and store it where it would not get beaten up by the North Country's severe winter weather. It was on a cold November night that we got the vessel in condition to travel across the lake to Plattsburgh. Shortly after leaving Burlington, an awning dropped over the side and became tangled in one propeller. Using only one engine, we managed to get the vessel to Plattsburgh, and tied the old vessel up at my dock. After freeing the propeller, we took her up to Monty's Bay and berthed her there for the winter.

That winter the vessel filled with ice and it took an awful toll on the old boat. During this time, one of the vessel's previous owners – who apparently had some sort of mental problem – was at the ferry landing over in Vermont and drove his car off into the lake. He was pulled from the icy water but died about a week later of hypothermia. The boat's new owner was unable to pay me for my salvage work and the *Mount Independence* wound up in my ownership. Eventually, I sold the boat, and through the sale, recovered what I had invested in its salvage. The man who purchased the *Mount Independence* from me advised that he was going to take it down to Baltimore, Maryland and from there, he was going down to St. Croix. That year the island had been devastated by hurricane Hugo and apparently there was a lot of money to be made down there doing repair work in the harbors. I immediately recognized the opportunity. to make some money while enjoying the tropics, so I took my whole crew to St. Croix. I believe it was either 1988 or 1989 and we had such a good time that we made the visit to the island an annual trip. When we arrived in St. Croix, we went to work for a company by the name of *Balfour Beatty,* which was out of Liverpool England. During the day we worked at a variety of things. One of our projects was rebuilding the Fredericstrad dock, which required considerable time underwater. Diving in the blue-green warm tropical water was a pleasurable experience and there were a lot of interesting fish and other creatures that we thrilled at seeing. Evenings we had a great time visiting a place on top of a mountain that went by the name, *Domino Club.* A specialty of the club was 'pig on a spit' and for $5 you got to eat all the pork you could eat and all the rum you could drink. However, we had to bring our own mixer for the rum. As everyone probably knows, rum is the preferred drink in the Caribbean and I was amazed at how cheap it was. We could purchase a quart of rum for $1.29 and we'd do a breakfast special, which consisted of a half glass of rum and quarter glass of orange juice. Ironically, the orange juice cost more than the rum."

While managing the marina, we did a lot of salvage work. We rescued boats that broke free from their mooring. We also frequently went out on the lake to search for boaters who were reported missing. That was one of the functions that led to my being asked to head up the Sheriff's boat patrol. A woman would call us and report 'my husband went out on the lake fishing this morning and he hasn't come home.'

We went looking for him and in most instances – like that – we learned the fisherman husband had tied up at a bar somewhere on shore, got loaded and was having such a good time, he forgot what time it was. That was the case four or five times. Sometimes, boats were wrecked in storms and we salvaged them. We had primitive equipment, but I had learned a lot about marine salvage when I worked for Merritt-Chapman & Scott, so we were pretty successful, despite our equipment."

Sometimes Frank was called upon to perform difficult work at lakeside and the steep terrain in some of the locations presented quite a challenge. Such was the case when a portion of railroad tracks washed out, causing a train to derail in a steep area of terrain near Port Douglas.

Frank relates, "A few years ago, we had severe rains and a heavy water run-off from the mountains washed out a section of railroad track down in Port Douglas. A train came along, hit the washout and derailed. Fifteen cars rolled down an embankment. I was contacted by the railroad and hired to work with them in repairing the track along the embankment at lakeside. At that time I owned a tug and barge on which I loaded an escavator and we went down to Port Douglas. The railroad had been unable to access the section of track that needed repair and my equipment solved that problem. We pulled in to various points where we could run up on shore with the escavator; the railroad was able to do the repairs using my equipment, which saved them a lot of money and which pleased them very much. We were called to help the railroad out again when a small earthquake hit the area and derailed a train down in Port Henry. Two carloads of cement and five carloads of lumber had tumbled off the tracks. We went down with the tug and barge and recovered floating lumber and debris from the waters of Lake Champlain."

The word spread that if you needed a job done on Lake Champlain, Frank Pabst was the man you wanted to call and consequently, Frank was frequently called upon for work associated with the lake.

Frank recalls, "In the 1980's Mobil Oil wanted me to remove an oil dolphin for them down in Westport. I took the Juniper down along with a crane I had purchased from Marble Island. How I came into ownership of the crane is rather interesting. I had signed a contract with Freddy Fayette, who owned Marble Island and also owns Juniper Island. Freddy also owns the search boat used by the Lake Champlain

Maritime Museum. Freddy Fayette ended up selling Marble Island to a guy named Judd, who bought the *Intrepid Yacht*, which was the winner of the American cup race one year. While at Marble Island, I noticed an old crane sitting beside the water. It was in terrible condition, but I needed a crane and I asked Judd how much he wanted for it. Judd said the crane was no longer of value to him and he would sell it to me at the price presently being offered for scrap steel. I had my engineer put a battery in the crane and we fired it up. The crane had a Jimmy diesel engine, which we were able to start. It ran beautifully! Everything else was stiff on it, but it managed to swing, turn, crawl, hoist and lower. I was thrilled to have purchased a crane so cheaply. Judd had said he would take $500 for the crane. The next day I went to pay him the $500 and he told me that he hadn't realized that the crane would still start and function. I told him that the crane just needed some TLC and when we gave it, it performed well.

"Well," Judd responded, "when I offered it to you for $500, I didn't know it was operable. As it is obviously operable, I've got to get more money for it."

"He was obviously trying to welsh on the deal we had struck and it made me angry, but I bit my tongue and asked, so how much more money do you want?"

Judd responded, "I need another $500."

"I forked over the additional $500 and was preparing to leave when some flat bed trucks showed up loaded with material that needed unloading."

Judd asked, "How much would it cost me for you to unload those flatbeds with the crane?"

"I forced back a smile as I responded, I will need $600 to unload them."

Judd agreed and added, "You know there are five moorings that need to be removed which are not on our contract. How much do you want to move the moorings?"

Again, I forced back a smile and responded, "It will be $1000, which comes out to $200 per mooring. Judd accepted, so I essentially got the crane free. All it cost me was the work we invested in it. Anyway, we got the crane loaded on a Lake Champlain Transportation Company barge and towed the barge to Westport with the *Juniper*. We tied up to the Dolphin (pier used by oil barges) that needed removal and went to work. I had a small hydraulic chain saw and a small bobcat with a hydraulic port to run the chain saw. Brad Knapp was my diver on the project and I had another two men on deck to load sections that we removed. The Dolphin pier timbers were 12 inches square and 16 feet long. We started ripping them apart and as we got down below the water, we discovered the dolphin was filled with stone and fill. That necessitated breaking this down to remove the timbers. It was quite a task, but we finally removed the timbers and all that was left was a small pile of stones scattered on the lake bottom. The Department of Environmental Conservation inspected our work and found it acceptable. For about two weeks work, I cleared about $25,000, and I expressed to Mobil Oil that they should feel free to call me for any sort of work around Lake Champlain."

Mabel Smith Douglass

Although most of the *Wreck Raider's* dives were in Lake Champlain, perhaps the dive they would become most publicly noted for started out as a routine training mission. As it turned out, it would be far from routine. *Plattsburgh Press-Republican* reporter Jeff Meyers did an excellent job of reporting the story in the edition of September 20, 2003, and titled the piece, *"Placid Drowning of Yore Evokes Vivid Memories."* Mr. Meyers relates, "It was one of those pleasant late-summer afternoons. The deep-blue sky felt warm, despite a chill in the air that said autumn was approaching. Frank Pabst had promised a special day for the half-dozen young men who were learning how to dive safely and professionally. The group had traveled to Lake Placid for some clear diving in the lake's cool, deep water."

"We were looking for any kind of underground connection between Lake Placid and the Ausable River," said Pabst, now the retired skipper of Juniper Boat Tours in Plattsburgh and long-time marine salvager. "In reality, we just used that as an excuse to go diving."

"It was 40 years ago, Sept. 15, 1963. Pabst, in his 30's at the time, had taken the young divers under his wing. The year-ending trip to Lake Placid was one way he could show them his appreciation for their efforts."

"They were all young men who enjoyed diving," Pabst said. "The water in Lake Placid was so incredibly clear, I thought they'd enjoy the experience from having a few deep dives there."

"The group, calling itself the Lake Champlain Wreck Raiders, often searched for historical artifacts that members had identified through research. Randy Larkin, 17 at the time, remembers that they were interested in a boat (as reported) that might have been lost near

Pulpit Rock years earlier. The lake plunges 90 feet off a sheer drop from the edge of Pulpit Rock. Even at those depths, the visibility was pronounced, and divers could see several feet in front of them as they made their way along the lonely bottom. The men had decided to dive in pairs as they searched the underwater cliffs for a portal through the mountain to the river on the other side or for remnants of the wagon (as reported). At 90-plus feet, they could stay under water only for about 15 minutes. Jimmy Rogers and Dick Niffenegger were first to enter the liquid realm. Following the submerged cliff of Pulpit Rock, they headed for the lake bottom, an area where no living person had probably been before. On their way, the pair found an old guide boat perched on a ledge of the cliff about halfway down. They also uncovered a rusty hatchet at the base of the cliff. So they weren't that startled when they came across what looked to be a department-store mannequin lying on the bottom about 60 feet from the cliff."

"When they first saw it, their first thought was to play a joke on the rest of us by bringing it up to the surface claiming they'd found a body," Pabst said.

"But when the two divers looked more closely, they realized that what they had found actually was a human body. Niffenegger, a sergeant from the Air Force, motioned for Rogers to stay with the body while he resurfaced to tell the others."

"When he first surfaced, our immediate thoughts were that he was making it up, but it didn't take us long to realize he was telling the truth," Pabst recalled of the intense tone the diver had used. "Jimmy was a kid of 18," he added. "He was left down there alone and had started feeling uncomfortable. So he grabbed the body and started back up."

"As the other divers prepared to enter the lake, they noticed that Rogers was moving up toward the air bubbles popping the lake's surface. Larkin was one of the young men who jumped in to meet him halfway up the water column."

"The body was well preserved, but once Jimmy started bringing her up, she started disintegrating," said Larkin, now a local automobile dealer. "It's pretty cold down that deep, and, with the minerals down there, there wasn't a lot of deterioration."

"An autopsy performed later revealed that the body's outer layers had formed into a hard, wax-like coating, but the internal organs were nearly as fresh as the day the woman died. By the time the men had it secured, an arm and the head had become detached. Although they were able to retrieve the head, they never found the arm. A jawbone that had fallen off was found a few days later."

Larkin and the others were stunned by the discovery, but they already had experience with body recoveries from other drownings. "I'd already picked up a dozen bodies on rescue operations," Larkin said. "We weren't looking for it, but it wasn't that traumatic finding the body."

"Larkin, whose family owned the area's first diving shop in Plattsburgh, was already a veteran diver and had been on several deep-water dives before the Lake Placid trip. But the find made an impression on him that lasts to this day.

"I'll never forget that day," he said. "It was a beautiful day. The water was very clear, but it was quite cold down there, maybe 35 degrees."

Wreck Raiders

Pulpit Rock

Over the next few days, the mystery of this unusual find was slowly uncovered. In the collective memory of several local people, only one woman had ever drowned in the lake and had not been found: Anna Mabel Smith Douglass. The autopsy and subsequent reports verified that the woman was indeed Douglass, former Dean of Douglass College for women in New Jersey, who owned a camp on Lake Placid about 2 ½ miles from Pulpit Rock. Niffenegger and Rogers brought another bit of information to the surface that cleared up a lot of the mystery about Douglass's fate. When first discovering the body, the divers noted that a rope was tied around the woman's neck and was attached to a horse anchor on the other end. When they touched the rope, however, it disintegrated, and the anchor slipped into the deep mulch of the lake bottom. During subsequent dives, Pabst and his crew could not find the anchor again. Larkin remembers being called out of class one day to return to the site for a deep-water dive (state troopers were not allowed to dive below 55 feet at the time). Douglass had disappeared almost 30 years to the day before the Wreck Raiders had uncovered her watery grave. On Sept. 21, 1933, she had gone onto the lake for one last row before leaving Lake Placid for the summer. A search for the woman, who had been suffering a nervous breakdown and resigned her position as dean at the college, proved fruitless, and the memory of the incident slowly faded into memory (as reported). But the Wreck Raiders' find opened a new investigation that ultimately led to a decision that her death was an accident. The idea of suicide – and even murder – became the fodder for legends about a woman whose life ended tragically in the cold, dark depths of the unknown."

The story so intrigued Captain Pabst's friend New York Assemblyman Chris Ortloff, a resident of Plattsburgh, that he wrote and published the story in a book titled, *"A Lady In The Lake – The True Account of Death and Discovery in Lake Placid."*

Frank has vivid recall of that memorable day at Lake Placid in 1963 and is quick to point out "Although the Coroner ruled her death was an accident, I maintain that she was murdered. Of course 30 years had passed since she was killed and it was a lot easier for authorities to close the case by agreeing that her death resulted from an accident or suicide. How logical is it that this wealthy woman clad in a black dress and wearing a hat, with veil attached, is going to go out for a spin on Lake Placid alone, in a guide boat that was powered by oars? How logical is it that a woman who never lifted anything heavier than a pencil, tied the boat's anchor rope around her neck, then lifted a 50pound anchor and threw it over the side of the boat? Our divers were positive they saw the rope around her neck and the anchor, but as the state police wouldn't dive below 50 feet, they couldn't confirm our findings at 95 feet. I don't know how 'they' justified a verdict of accidental death."

Captain Frank The Environmentalist

Over the years, many politicians and North Country residents were under the misguided impression that former junkyard operator Frank Pabst was a lake scavenger unconcerned about preserving the beauty and environment of the magnificent body of water. They probably arrived at this conclusion after viewing the condition of the Captain's business property located in the D & H railroad yard at lakeside.

The truth is, Frank Pabst fell in love with Lake Champlain at first sight and he explains with a chuckle, "I think Ann, who is the epitome of honesty and virtue would attest that I was more devoted to the care and custody of the Lake Champlain environment than I was to the care and custody of my family. The reason my boatyard looked so decrepit was because I was always operating on a shoestring budget and, therefore, I purchased boats and marine salvage equipment that looked like they were ready for the scrap yard, but I salvaged pieces and parts from them to keep my operable boats and equipment going. My yard was a real mess, but, hey, I was working out of a railroad yard, which is messy looking anyway. Only folks who really didn't know me complained that I was destroying the environment, or that I didn't care about preserving the lake. The truth is, I don't think there is a man alive who cares more about keeping Lake Champlain clean and beautiful and I can offer proof of this attestation. Of course, like any other good businessman, if aiding the environment resulted in my making a few bucks, that was a plus. Over the years, I turned down work that I considered would be damaging to the lake's environment. Some of my detractors will disagree and bring up the fact that when legislation was proposed that would require all boats to have closed circuit marine toilets I protested against it. Actually, I believed that requiring boats to have closed toilets was a good thing, but I opposed the legislation at that time because I felt that rather than taking on the cities of Plattsburgh and Burlington, which dumped as much waste in the lake in one day as all the boats operating on the lake would have dumped in it in ten years, the politicians focused on just boaters. Their attitude seemed to be, 'if you owned a boat, you were rich, so let's get all these rich guys to pay for clean up of the lake. Well, it didn't work that way. The legislation passed and it helped a little bit, but over time – as preserving the environment grew in importance – sewage coming into the lake was regulated and the lake is a much healthier environment than it was forty years ago. The Lake Champlain Preservation Committee is doing a good job. The thing that concerns me about rabid environmentalists is that they carry their issues to the extreme and force higher taxes on everyone. They sometimes also defy logic and good sense. For example, the problem of run-off of fertilizers and animal excrement from farmlands abutting the lake continues to be a contentious issue. However, the same group ignores an environmental problem that I – for one – have pointed out on numerous occasions. The day before President Kennedy was shot, in 1963, the tugboat *William McAllister* headed out of Plattsburgh, towing a full barge. The *McAllister* struck Ferris Rock and the collision tore an 18" gash in the side of the tug. The gash was about 8' below the water line. For some reason – because they shouldn't have been traveling that way – they had all the ship compartments open and the boat sank in just seven minutes. As the last man on board scrambled up the hawsers, he chopped the lines free that connected the barge, probably thinking that doing so would save the barge. Personally, I believe this was a mistake, because if they had kept the hawsers in place, they may have saved the tug. In any event, Hector and I dove on the site a week later. I photographed the tug for the insurance company and kept a copy of the photos for myself. Unfortunately, the photos burned in the fire we had in 1984. The *William McAllister* sank in 150' of water, and its condition on the bottom was weird and sort of dangerous. Apparently the boat's fire hoses had been coiled loosely alongside the cabin and when the boat sank, the hoses – which were filled with air – uncoiled and were undulating above the wreck, like the snakes that were Medusa's hairdo.

Divers who have explored the wreck in recent years report the hoses have rotted away, so the Medusa effect is gone. The *McAllister*, had between 6-10 thousand gallons of fuel oil on board when it went down over 40 years ago. Someday, those tanks are going to rust through and that oil is going to surface in the lake. I've told the state about it and I've told the Lake Champlain Committee about it. Incredibly, both agencies responded to me with the denial that the wreck exists and therefore there is no danger of pollution from it. Even after showing them newspaper clippings about the sinking and showing them a sonar picture of the tug lying on the bottom, they deny its existence. I know it is possible to remove that fuel oil before it escapes into the lake and none of the 'so-called' environmental protection groups appear interested in getting it done."

An underwater discovery by a politician snorkeling along the shore of Lake Champlain, would result in Frank being hired for an environmental cleanup project that put some dollars in his pocket and coincidentally saved the taxpayers a lot of money.

Reflection on that incident invokes another chuckle from a man who chuckles easily and often. He related, "It seems that one day, Vermont Senator Patrick Leahy went snorkeling in the vicinity of a lighthouse, near the shore of Vermont, and he came upon a large battery lying on the lake bottom. The Senator reported his finding to the Coast Guard who informed him that for many years it had been standard operating procedure for them to dispose of spent batteries that had powered the lighthouse light, by flinging them into the lake. Their attitude was, 'out of sight, out of mind.' So, it was determined that all of the lighthouses on the lake had a nest of batteries around the base of them, in the lake. Whether truly concerned that the batteries endangered the lake's environment, or, looking to gain a lot of votes by making the batteries an environmental issue, the Senator directed that the batteries had to be removed from the lake. No batteries had been disposed of in the lake in about 30years, because it was that long ago that the Coast Guard placed solar powered lights in all the lighthouses. I suspect that as protecting the environment was a very big issue at the time, the Senator's raising an outcry about the batteries and ordering their removal was more about getting votes than protecting the lake. Anyway, the Coast Guard contacted me and I was asked to take an investigating firm out to examine ten lighthouses at the southern end of the lake and see how extensive the battery problem was. They counted approximately 50batteries, a report was filed and it was decided they should be removed. Personally, I felt that as the batteries had been on the bottom for 30-40 years, anything that was going to leach out of them had already done so. In my opinion those batteries were just as much a part of Lake Champlain as the nasty zebra mussels are now. After learning that the 'environmental cleanup' of batteries from the lake was going to occur, I kept my eyes and ears open for the announcement of where to submit bids to obtain the contract. A few months went by and nothing seemed to be happening on this, so I called the Coast Guard Commander over in Burlington and asked what was going on."

"Oh, that contract has been awarded," he informed me.

"How did that happen?" I asked. "I have been watching the Plattsburgh and Burlington papers for the announcement of proposed bids and didn't see it appear?"

The Commander responded, "Well, it wasn't announced because we don't have to request bids for projects under $500,000 and we were informed that the contract had to be awarded to a minority-owned contracting company."

"Needless to say, I smelled something fishy was going on and I wasn't standing by the water while the Coast Guard Commander was telling me this. I wasn't going to let the Commander off the hook without getting all the details, so I asked, who, or what company was awarded the contract?"

"It was Jason & Associates," he replied.

"After learning this, I did some research and found out that Jason & Associates was being run by a Hawaiian who held a PHD in nuclear physics. He holds himself out to be a minority and bids on construction projects all over the United States. At the time the government had been directed to award a certain number of contacts to minority businesses. I learned that Jason & Associates had bid as a minority owned company and obtained the contract for fuel remediation on the Plattsburgh Air Force Base. He was paid $500,000 for that job. He actually (after receiving the contract) paid a local contractor $250,000 to do the work and he pocketed the other $250,000. After learning this information, I re-contacted the Coast Guard Commander and asked him how much the government was going to pay Jason & Associates for the battery removal contract."

"The contract is for $500,000," he responded.

"Hearing this made me angry because paying a half million bucks to remove a few batteries from shallow water was ridiculous. I counted to ten and then told the Commander that spending that amount of money for such a simple job amounted to theft from the taxpayers. You know, I added, all you would have to do is put out the word to scuba divers that you would pay them ten bucks for every battery they pulled out of the lake and they would be removed in short order."

His response was, "Well, this removal has to be done in an environmentally safe manner."

"That answer didn't make any more sense to me than his previous answers because the most environmentally safe method of retrieving the batteries was by scuba divers. I could see that I wasn't getting anywhere with the Commander, so I pursued the issue up the Coast Guard chain of command. I eventually got the ear of the Admiral in Charge of the Coast Guard, and pressured him as to how come the contract was let without bid. He repeated what had been told to me by the local Commander. He was given orders that the contract was to be awarded to a minority owned contracting company, and someone in the bureaucracy awarded the contract to Jason & Associates. I informed him that $500,000 was far too much to pay for the removal, that the whole process smelled rotten and that I suspected someone was getting their hands greased for awarding the contract to a specific company. I also informed him that I intended to go public and someone's feet would be held to the fire. The next thing I knew, the contract was pulled and the batteries were removed from the lake by a group of Army Corps of Engineers stationed at Fort Eustes, Virginia. I was contracted to provide the equipment the Corps of Engineers used for the removal. We started down at White Hall and worked our way north along the lake. When the batteries were brought up, they were placed in an - 'official' - environmentally safe container - 10 to a container. Then the container was sealed and delivered to some place in Buffalo. I don't know how Buffalo got so lucky, but that is where they went. We removed 9-tons of batteries from the waters of Lake Champlain and I charged the Coast Guard about $40,000 for our services, which consisted of two weeks work for myself and crewmen and the use of my tug and barge. As the Corps of Engineers consisted of military personnel, their service didn't cost anything. The job saved the taxpayers a lot of money and, probably, some bureaucrat is still cussing me for denying him a pay off. We had a good time with the Corps of Engineer divers, and while they were here I told them about the *William McAllister* and I was told that they had removed fuel from a sunken wreck in Lake Erie and would be able to remove the fuel oil from the *McAllister* if they were directed to do so.''

In the early 1960's Frank took on management of the Valcour Marina.

He relates, "At the time, I was still driving the bread route for Bouyea Bakery, operating my dive shop and very involved with the *Wreck Raiders,* diving and training divers. Bill Reid owned the Valcour Marina, where my dive shop was located and he sold the Marina to an Air Force Colonel stationed at Plattsburgh Air Force Base. The Colonel asked me to manage the Marina. At the time, I was driving to Lake Placid every morning, delivering bread and left Plattsburgh at 4:00 a.m. I was back in Plattsburgh by 2:00 p.m. and went down to the marina. The marina office was located in a three-story building located at lakeside. Bill Reid had operated a 'Tastee-Freeze' ice cream outlet on the first level when he owned the marina. When I took over the operation for the Colonel, we closed the Tastee-Freeze and I moved my dive shop into that portion of the building. Having my dive shop and manager's office in the same building made it easier for me to run the operation. Today, the building is owned by the owners of Snug Harbor Marina and leased as the Harborside Restaurant. Things were going along fairly well, until we started getting burgled. Over the course of a few months the building was broken into twice and we lost about a thousand bucks in cash and merchandise with each break-in. The burglaries were reported to the State Police but they didn't seem to have any luck catching the burglar(s) and so I decided to booby trap the place. During this same time period, I was involved in negotiation to open another dive shop on the pier over in Burlington. In order to get permission to locate there, I had to remove some old salt dock pilings. After studying the situation, I decided the quickest and easiest way to dispose of the pilings was with explosives. I acquired a supply of RDX and primer cord, attached a small charge to each piling at the mud line and clipped them off by setting off the charge. It worked fine. Using the explosives for this gave me the bright idea on how I could put an end to the burglaries of our Marina in Valcour. I placed a grape sized ball of RDX on the inside wall at about testicle level, inserted an electric blasting cap and wired the cap to contacts placed on the upper corner of the window. If the window were pried open, a metal contact on the edge of the window would make contact with a contact placed in the track, creating a spark that would set off the cap. I came in one morning to discover the window and about three courses of concrete block below it blown out. The burglar(s) apparently came by boat, because I found a small trail of blood leading from the blast site to where a boat had been tied up. When the state police saw what happened, they chuckled, but chastised me for my method of invoking instant justice. Apparently, whatever injury the burglar(s) received from my little surprise, were not too serious, because they didn't show up at a hospital and were never arrested. Of course we had to repair the damage caused by the blast, but imagining the look of shock, surprise and pain on the low-life thief's face as the window he was prying open exploded, made it well worth it. I also like to believe the shocking experience made the fellow seek a more honest career.

While I was managing the Valcour Marina, my son Eric, who was about 8 or 9 years old at the time, hung out at the marina and performed small tasks for boaters who then tipped him. One of the marina members happened to be President of the sailing club and he was a very obnoxious person. He was constantly complaining about everything and no matter what we did, we couldn't please him. One of the things that Eric did was take people out to their boats that were tied up on a mooring in the harbor, using the marina rowboat. He made pretty good tips doing this and that one summer he made a couple hundred bucks, which was a considerable amount of money for a little kid. Anyway, one day Eric came to me in tears and told me that 'Mr. Obnoxious member' had given him a hard time. I paid 'Mr. Obnoxious' – who in addition to being President of the sailing club was a rather influential businessman in town – a visit. I informed him that he and his boat were to leave the property immediately and if he didn't leave on his own, I would cut his boat loose and set it adrift. Well, he left in a huff and went up to Plattsburgh. When he found out what it would cost him to moor at the 'Dock and Coal' marina in the city, he returned to Valcour much more humble. He apologized for his treatment of Eric and told me if we let him back in the marina, he would be sure to tip my son every Sunday. I let him back and the following Sunday, when he appeared at the marina, he held up a dime and said, 'see, my wife made sure I brought money to tip your son.' I was sure his display was a form of sarcasm, but in any event, from that day on, he was happy, my son was happy and he stayed as a member of Valcour Marina."

By 1968, everyone having an affinity for Lake Champlain knew that Frank Pabst was the man to see regarding just about anything having to do with the lake. Joan Clark was one of those people and, after receiving a settlement resulting from the death of her husband (from the result of) an automobile accident in Montreal, she decided to settle in Valcour and purchased a commercial campground located on the lake at Snug Harbor. Joan asked Frank if he would manage the campground and he agreed.

Frank relates, "Joan was a wonderful woman and, after the tragic loss of her husband, she purchased a popular campground for campers with house trailers or self contained R.V.s. Joan asked me to manage the campground and I couldn't say no. We had some interesting times there and eventually, I convinced her to let me convert the campground into a marina. When I started, the campground had twenty-five available slots with hookup for utilities and sewage. At first it appeared that we weren't going to get any business for our first summer season, because we weren't getting any calls. Then, out-of-the-blue, I received a call from a Mr. Gregory or Gregoire, who said he wanted to rent all twenty-five slots. He accepted the rental price that I quoted and we struck a deal. On the day Gregory or Gregoire arrives, he pulls in driving a new Lincoln, towing a Holiday Rambler trailer and he is followed by a train of cars pulling trailers, and pickup trucks carrying spray tanks. When they pulled in, I said to myself, *'oh-oh, this is a band of gypsies and we are in for trouble.* I was immediately concerned as to what we would be missing when they left and what they would do to our reputation in the community. However, Gregory, or Gregoire, their leader, had paid in cash and a deal was a deal. They parked their trailers, settled in and stayed with us for about two-weeks. During the day the men traveled about the North Country spraying driveways, roofs and garages with whatever concoction they had in the tanks on their trucks. We had a few problems with them and I quickly learned the easiest way to resolve any issue was by going directly to Mr. Gregory or Gregoire. A very amusing thing happened while the gypsies were with us and it involved our garbage man. We had contracted with a local trash collector to pick up the garbage at the campground. The nice enough fellow happened to have a speech impediment. His S came out as a T when he spoke and, if he was excited, his lisping became more pronounced. What happened was that the gypsies were killing live chickens and disposing of the innards, heads and feathers in the 55-gallon trash barrels we had placed throughout the grounds. Our trash man appeared in the marina office and he was obviously upset. He wanted to borrow a snow shovel from us and he was so excited, this is what I heard him say:

"Thoth damned gypthy thud be thent back to Thekovakia, or wherever thay came from! They ith heathenth! They makin' a damn thinkin' meth killin' chikenth and throwin' dare guth in da thrath!"

"I did my best to keep from laughing at the poor fellow and asked him what he needed a snow shovel for."

He responded, "Damned jethable (jezebel) bared her hairy ath right in front of me and made me thill a barrel of guth on the ground! I need a thuvel to clean the meth up."

"By this time I was taking deep breaths to hold back laughter and tears were coming to my eyes. I knew what he was saying but I wondered why one of the gypsy women would do such a thing. So I asked, "How did she expose herself to you?"

His eyes were wide with excitement as he sputtered, "Thie twatted down right in front of me, pulled up her dreth and pithed! Made me thill the barrel and made a thinking meth all over. I need a thnow thovel to clean it up!"

"I found a snow shovel for the poor fellow and when he left, I laughed so hard my stomach hurt, and those who know me, know that is a considerable expanse of hurt. One had to have been there to appreciate the humor of the moment. I cannot do justice in describing the look on the fellow's face and the animation of his body as he lisped his dilemma. I am forced to laugh when I recall that moment. Anyway, the gypsies stayed for a couple of weeks and then moved on. I can imagine they kept looking for new areas to scavenge and were staying a few steps in front of the law.

Our campground was located very near the south end of the runway serving Plattsburgh Air Force Base. Consequently, planes landing or taking off passed very low overhead. Sometimes when people stopped to inquire about renting a campsite, a jet happened to take off or land. If they expressed concern, I would laugh and jokingly tell them, 'Don't worry about the planes, they're on our side.' My little joke worked on some, but others responded, 'Well, I can't sleep with that noise over my head,' and they left.

As the campground was located at lakeside on one of the most scenic and historic coves on Lake Champlain, I recognized the potential of turning the camp into a combined marina/campground. Joan agreed and in short order Snug Harbor Marina and Campground was doing a thriving business. We managed to attract a lot of boat owners who were berthed in Plattsburgh, to come down and join us because we charged a lot less money and Snug Harbor is only about four miles south of the city. Soon we had a waiting list of boaters wanting to use our facilities and it was necessary to keep adding docking and mooring buoys for sailboats."

Television Personality

While managing Snug Harbor, Frank continued driving his bread route for Bouyea Bakery in order to support his growing family. Having more mouths to feed, bodies to clothe and needing the essentials for the care of infants and toddlers, motivated Frank to continue seeking ways to improve his income. His dream was to eventually own and operate his own business; however, that goal was frustrated by the lack of funds to get a business up and running. Ever ambitious, he worked at many jobs and was not afraid to tackle a job that seemed beyond the scope of his intellect and ability. Surprising to some folks – but not to those who really knew him – Frank quickly learned the skills required for the particular job he was hired for and continually honed those skills to improve his performance.

In inimitable style Frank explains, "I've got a great line of b---s--- and have always been able to find a solution to any problem, although I must admit that I quietly buried a lot of mistakes along the way. Many of my solutions flew contrary to acceptable governmental or bureaucratic standards but - what the heck, my philosophy is to hell with red tape. Let's get the job done!"

Although proud of his German heritage, the Korean War veteran was even more proud to be an American, and considered himself blessed to be living in the beautiful Champlain Valley, that despite its immensity was only a miniscule part of the great nation known as the United States of America, which was truly a land of opportunity for those willing to take the risk and invest time and energy.

Normally smiling blue eyes quickly turn to ice and an accompanying uplifted chin present a warning to anyone who dare's challenge Frank's patriotism or love for his country and he feels no compassion for "unpatriotic ignoramuses" who defile or destroy the national ensign and demonstrate against the military.

He readily attests, "This nation has given so much to the Pabst family. In what other nation on earth could a stubborn, free spirited kid drop out of school and go on to achieve so much happiness and success. I love this country and I consider myself very patriotic! I suppose my German heritage contributes to my stubbornness, but I am only stubborn when I know I am right. Anyway, when 1960 rolled in, the Korean War was over and our nation was at peace. Ann and I were extremely happy, our family was growing and, although we didn't have any money in the bank, I was gainfully employed. All of these things made me optimistic that the era of the 60's would be prosperous – not just for the Pabst family – but the nation as a whole. Living in my beautiful little corner of the North Country, I did not foresee, nor anticipate, the Vietnam War, or its resulting tragic loss of life, how it would create a bitter divide in America and assail the strong sense of patriotism that kept our nation unified and strong for nearly 200 years. Actually, the Vietnam War did not personally affect our family; however, like thousands of other Americans, we watched the news and were saddened and dismayed by the assassination of President Kennedy. We were dismayed and outraged by the criminal antics, anti-war protests and treasonous conduct occurring throughout America, and saddened at how all of this outrage was tearing apart the framework of morality and patriotism that made our nation strong. I perceived the shenanigans of the anti-war protestors as intended to lower the morale of our military. By now, everyone reading this has begun to wonder why a dissertation on the Vietnam War is included in the telling of my life story, if the war didn't touch us in some fashion? Well, indirectly, it did, because at the time I was working in a job that I enjoyed very much. My stubborn patriotism and need to publicly convey my feelings resulted in my receiving a reprimand, in the form of a format change, from my employer. Needless to say, I did not accept this chastisement gracefully and what had hitherto been a wonderful workplace suddenly changed into a hostile work environment. For a time I kept my frustration and anger in check, held my tongue and did not voice my true feelings. Those who know me realize just how difficult it was for me to remain silent. However, one morning my head was rebelling from a night of 'spirited imbibing' while conducting business, and I was in no mood to accept a tongue-lashing from anyone. I must admit that spouting off with my mouth was bad enough, but adding emphasis with my fist was somewhat over-zealous. Needless to say, that uninhibited behavior ended my employment as a TELEVISION PERSONALITY. Okay, so I have a reputation for spinning yarns and tales and it sounds incredible that a salty tongued rascal like me could ever host a television show, but it's true folks and those natives of Plattsburgh, who were around during that era may recall *Country Corner* which aired on WPTZ television, hosted by Frank Pabst. This is the story of that misadventure in my life. I was busy at driving my bread route, managing Snug Harbor Marina, diving with the *Wreck Raiders* and doing some lake salvage. One day, Mel Luck, a sportscaster on WPTZ Channel 5 television was at the marina and I mentioned to him that I needed to find another line of work that would produce more income. Mel told me that WPTZ had an opening for a 'switcher' and said that if I applied for the position, he would give me a recommendation. I knew absolutely nothing about 'switching' and asked Mel to explain what the job entailed. He told me that a 'switcher' sits in the control room at the studio and was responsible for switching from on-air programming to commercial segments and back to programming again. It sounded like something I could handle, so I applied for the position and was hired. I quickly learned that the work of a switcher didn't require physical labor – which was a plus – and that it was actually quite enjoyable. Making it all the more enjoyable was the fact that all the folks at WPTZ were friendly, they all treated me with respect and it was just a fun place to work. Within short order, my handsome face, wonderful physique, superior intellect, wonderful personality and gift of gab, apparently impressed the leadership of the station. The station manager told me that WPTZ needed to fill a half-hour slot in the early a.m. and had decided to introduce a Country-Western music show. He asked me if I would be interested in hosting the show. I have always enjoyed country music and so I thought it was a great idea. I thanked him for placing such trust in my ability to host a television show and immediately said – yes. Thus it came to pass that *Country Corner* was born and I launched on a new career as a video disc jockey. *Country Corner* aired between nine and nine-thirty every weekday. The show was 'live' which meant that I had to make an attempt to look my best at an hour when I normally looked my worst. Pete Premo was my engineer. He was a great guy and we had a lot of fun. Pete was working his way through college at the time and in addition to being my program engineer, he was doing his own country-western show over in Saranac Lake for WNBZ, a Jimmy Rogers owned station. Pete's father, Henry Premo, was an engineer and responsible for maintaining the transmitter up on Terry Mountain, and was referred to as 'The Man of the Mountain. Pete and I were always playing tricks on each other. Pete would sneak up in front of me while I was on-air and he pulled my desk away from the camera. He, and others, tried to get me to have a sour face while I was on-air by sucking on lemons in front of me. That didn't work, because I rather enjoy lemons, especially when they are in a martini. They pulled all sort of antics and we had a wonderful time."

Pete (Pierre) Premo confirms that he enjoyed working with Frank at Channel 5 offering, "Frank has the gift of gab and kind of personality that attracts people. As host of *Country Corner* he played music from taped performances and pulled in some local bands to give them recognition. Frank had a lot of energy." Poking fun at Frank's girth he added, "If I wore one of Frank's shirts it would look like something I had purchased from Omar the tent maker."

In continued recollection on this phase of his life, Frank relates, "Being an early morning person and thoroughly enjoying my work, I arrived at the station at around 6:00 a.m. and kicked off the day for our faithful, patriotic viewers by playing the National Anthem and saluting the flag. As host of *Country Corner,* I introduced local music groups, bantered a little with them and they played a couple of songs. The management of the studio seemed to enjoy my droll humor and I was pretty much given free rein to create the show's format. I had a loyal, devoted audience that tuned in to *Country Corner* every morning and for the life of me, I don't know why. I frequently asked myself, *is the show that good or does my audience consist of bartenders and barflies who enjoy country music and can relate to Frank Pabst's on air antics and droll humor?* To this day, I am proud of the show's success. *Country Corner* was pulling down a Neilson 7 share rating as compared to the 3 - 5 share rating appreciated by the Merv Griffin and Mike Douglas shows which were on at the same time on competing networks. I guess management recognized my potential because I was asked to don a second hat and took on the responsibility of commercial sales representative for the station. This sometimes entailed working late hours in order to land a client. Switching hats from sales to host of *Country Corner,* then switcher, wasn't difficult; however, trying to look like a wide awake dream-boat after working on a potential sales client in a bar or restaurant most of the previous night, made it difficult. I would admit that a liberal consumption of dry martinis throughout the night added to that dilemma and I started many mornings with a bass drum pounding inside my head accompanied by a seemingly cotton filled mouth. I was putting in long hours for WPTZ, but I really enjoyed what I was doing and they seemed happy with me. Our proximity to the Canadian border meant much of our audience hailed from Canada. I was unaware as to how popular my show was up there until I was contacted by the owner of a popular, downtown, Montreal nightclub, who asked me if I would like to be a D.J. at the club on weekend evenings. It seemed an exciting adventure to me and I readily agreed. Of course, I didn't give much thought to my family at the time and it was quite selfish of me not to realize that as I would virtually be working seven days each week and wouldn't be home much. However, Ann actually seemed to enjoy the notoriety that was associated with my work at WPTZ, I was bringing in a decent paycheck and she recognized that I loved my work and we got along fine. Sometimes, after finishing my gig on St. Catherine Street in Montreal, I arrived back in Plattsburgh just in time to start the station off in the morning. Anyway, I was rolling along fat, dumb and happy in a career and doing things that I loved. As a Korean veteran and patriotic American, I believed that America went to war in Vietnam for the good cause of stopping Communist control and domination of Asian nations. I followed the daily negative news reports coming out of Vietnam, at first with aplomb, later with concern that forces within America were intent on destroying patriotism and in the process weakening the moral fiber that made our nation strong. I felt – and still feel to this day – that America would have been victorious in Vietnam if the war's direction had been taken out of the hand of politicians. Rather than taking the war to the enemy and defeating them, our troops were forced to maintain a defensive posture in a hostile environment, having an unstable and likely corrupt government. I was angry that the death of thousands of young Americans in Vietnam could be attributed to bungled political leadership and almost daily negative news reports that convinced our enemy that America was losing its resolve to defeat them. To me, anti-war demonstrations were a disgusting, unpatriotic display of ignorance by people who either didn't recognize or didn't care that their behavior was giving courage to the enemy, bolstering their resolve and indirectly causing the death of thousands of young soldiers.

There was a college homecoming planned at Plattsburgh State University at the time and it was reported that the administration had invited the Marine Drum and Bugle Corps to play in the homecoming day parade. A group of peaceniks, dreadniks, whatever they called themselves called a protest march, claiming that the marines were symbols of aggression and violence and should not be permitted on campus. The college President yielded to their protests and uninvited the Marine Corps Band. I was so angered by this that I did a six-minute, off the top of my head editorial, on air, one morning in which I criticized the college administration and stated that the protestors should get down on their knees and kiss the boots of the Marines for their heroic sacrifices. I said that if not for the heroism of our military America would not be the great and free nation that it is. Most of the viewers who saw my short tirade responded positively to the station. However, a handful of people protested to WPTZ management and I was called on the carpet. I was informed that as a result of my little diatribe, I would have to videotape my show and would no longer be doing a live performance. I argued that I preferred to do a live show because it offered spontaneity and I also knew that it took two-to-three hours to tape record a half hour show. But, they wouldn't budge. They did not want me doing live editorials on WPTZ. When I left the manager's office, I realized that the honeymoon was over as management had lost faith in me as a devoted, trusted employee and I was not happy with the way I was - in essence – being censored. I came into the station one morning hung over, after leaving the Surrey Lounge in Lake Placid at closing. I was at the Lounge trying to nail down a client for WPTZ, and, in fact, my night's work at the Surrey had picked up $25,000 in sales, so my condition was – in a way – work related. I came into work wearing cut-off sweats because after leaving the studio I intended to go diving, since going underwater in the lake usually cleared my head up. When I arrived, the Assistant Manager of the station called me into his office and gave me a ration of grief.

My head was pounding and I was in no mood for a lecture. My brain wasn't functioning too well, but there was nothing wrong with my mouth. I told him that I was in no mood for a lecture from him, but I foolishly emphasized my statement with my fist. I believe I hit him twice. That ended my career with WPTZ and I became a beer truck driver for Genesee beer for a short time. It is water over the dam now and long in my past, but I've got to admit that WPTZ was a wonderful experience and good time in my life.

Someone in Plattsburgh City government apparently appreciated my patriotism and my big mouth, or perhaps it was my work with the Sheriff's Department, because I was asked to take the job as Deputy Civil Defense Director for the City of Plattsburgh. I would wear a suit and go to my office in the daytime and then at six o'clock, I'd don coveralls, get behind the wheel of a four-axle truck and haul sludge from the sewer plant up to a landfill in Altoona. I did that for about two years, then, quit the civil defense job to run the *Juniper*. The civil defense position was a good job and I enjoyed it, but eventually, I felt guilty collecting my pay. Upon assuming the position, I put forth a supreme effort. I conducted an analysis of hazardous materials in the area; i.e. identified them, their hazardous nature, who possessed them, the quantity, where they were stored, etc. and I managed to put together a report consisting of about 60 pages. I was quite proud of what I had accomplished and when the Regional Director of Civil Defense came to Plattsburgh, I submitted it to him. He disinterestedly flipped through the pages of my report as one might flip through a deck of cards, then handed it back to me and said, 'That's great, where's the coffee pot?' It was only a short time before I came to the realization that I had become part of government bureaucracy. I held a position, was drawing a paycheck and was not expected to do anything. I became bored, paid scant attention to the job and was eager to look for another pasture. At the time, I gave considerable thought to the fact that Clinton County and Lake Champlain had a wealth of history and nobody was doing anything to preserve and promote it. Then I heard that Bill Scott had put the *Juniper* up for sale. I went off on a new adventure, and ended my association with the Civil Defense Commission."

Cliff Haven Cannons

On a warm Sunday in September 1968, teenage friends Patrick Munn, Mike Davidson and Peter Vernooy, residents of Cliff Haven, a small residential community on the west shore of Lake Champlain decided to go spear fishing. The boys were privileged to live in an area that not only presented one of the most beautiful vistas of Lake Champlain, but which was also steeped in history. Two major naval battles had taken place within sight of the Cliff Haven shoreline. A young Revolutionary leader by the name of Benedict Arnold, commanding a rag-tag fleet fought a pitched battle with a mighty British armada there in 1776, and a young American Commander by the name of James McDonough defeated an even mightier British Fleet in 1814. Standing on the lakeshore in Cliff Haven, the boys could readily observe the obelisk that had been erected on Crab Island - located about a mile off shore - to commemorate the island as a hospital and burying ground for participants killed during the engagement of 1814. Little did they anticipate as they entered the crystal clear water clad in swim suits, snorkel and fins, that they were about to embark on an adventure and make a discovery that would commence a controversy, which would go unresolved for many years. A controversy that would try the temerity and patience of Captain Frank Pabst, and result in personal disgust at the bureaucratic bungling and indecisiveness by state and local politicians. Frank became embroiled in the controversy by way of being a Good Samaritan and salvage operator interested in preserving the history of Lake Champlain.

According to the *Plattsburgh-Press-Republican* account of October 3, 1968, "It was a nice day and the waters of Lake Champlain were unusually clear, unveiling depths the boys had not explored.

The boys had been in the water only about ten minutes when it happened. It was after the boys had waded part way out and then headed further out toward an area where the water is about 15 feet deep.

Peter dove and came up yelling, "Sheephead." He had spotted a large fish, which he identified as being a Sheephead about 28 inches long. Quite a find, it roused the curiosity of the other swimmers. The large fish was believed headed in Mike's direction. Mike dove and came up yelling. But this time it wasn't the fish. It was something on the bottom of the lake. A cannon. The others didn't believe him, so Mike dove down again and this time he rapped his fist against the side of the ancient 12-pounder. Sure enough, it was a cannon. The boy's excitement mounted and…Pete dove, just about the time Pat was heading toward shore to summon help. Pete surfaced and excitedly proclaimed that he had found another cannon… Mike tied his red weight belt to one of the cannons marking the spot.

Pat managed to summon a small boat to the scene…and soon thereafter, a boat affectionately called "The Ark" pulled in and SCUBA divers went down to inspect the cannon more closely."

Pat Munn had been a member of "The Wreck Raiders" diving club, which had been created and was supervised by Captain Frank Pabst so once on shore he ran into his home and placed a call to Captain Frank's office. Wreck Raider diver Gary Brandstetter responded to Cliff Haven operating the "The Ark," which was the club's dive boat. After confirming that the boys had indeed located cannon on the lake bottom, Brandstter called Frank and requested other club members respond to aid in bringing the guns to the surface. The club's barge - more resembling a raft than a salvage vessel - was towed to the dive site using a small outboard boat operated by club members. The small homemade barge served as one of the Wreck Raiders first salvage barges. Mounted on the raft was a hand-operated crane, which owing to the size and ballast of the raft could retrieve objects of limited size from the lake bottom.

Cliff Haven Cannon

Frank recalls, "Raising the cannon with the small crane was difficult because they were quite heavy and partially buried in silt on the bottom of the lake. At one point the raft nearly flipped over trying to free the first cannon from the clutches of the lake. It took several hours to get both cannons aboard the raft. (In subsequent dives the group would also recover a large anchor from the Cliff Haven site) A quick examination of the approximately five feet long brass guns revealed one had been 'spiked' so that it could not be fired and the other had a cannon ball lodged in its barrel. Both guns had the date 1758 embossed on them. Now that the cannons were on board the raft, the question arose as to what to do with them. Word had begun to spread that an important historic find was taking place in the waters of Cliff Haven and the recovery operation attracted a small crowd. I personally believed that the cannons were state property, but should be kept in Plattsburgh for display. Those wishes were conveyed to the parents of the three boys, but in the meantime, members of a rival diving club known as the "Scuba Explorers" arrived and convinced the boys parents that the cannon were worth a lot of money and they should maintain control of them until being paid what they were worth. They poisoned the minds of the parents with the statement that the Wreck Raiders would exploit the discovery and cheat the boys out of their rightful monetary reward.

The raft was towed to our marina in Valcour, and the cannon off loaded into my pickup truck, for intended transfer to our museum on Miller Street in Plattsburgh. The parents of two of the boys and members of the Scuba Explorers opposed taking the cannons to our museum. When we arrived on my premises, the parents demanded that the cannons be returned to Cliff Haven and off loaded on the VerNooy lawn where they would be held as conversation pieces. I knew the cannon were a historic find and rightfully belonged to the state, so I refused. For a while we were in a 'Mexican standoff' and the atmosphere was quite tense. The parents were adamant that as their children had found the cannon, they had right of possession. I explained that state law provided that all lake salvage of historical value was the property of the state, but they had dollar signs in their eyes and became selectively deaf. They choose to listen to the Scuba Explorers encouragement that they could sell the cannons for a great sum of money, and would not listen to me. While we argued, members of the Scuba Explorers took it upon themselves to transfer the cannon from my pickup into one of their own. We made no attempt to stop them, because I figured after the state was notified, they would go to Cliff Haven and get them. The Scuba Explorers drove up to Cliff Haven and dumped the cannons on the front lawns of the Vernooy and Davidson residences."

Gary Brandstetter would later report in a letter published in the *Plattsburgh-Press Republican*, "We of the Wreck Raiders refuse to see such history flushed down a toilet like this and refused to deliver them to their homes. After being informed of these developments the State University said they would accept them."

In an interview by *the Plattsburgh-Press Republican*, Brandstetter related the complete details of how the Wreck Raiders became involved in the recovery and how the conflict as to right of possession originated. "One of the parents of the three boys who discovered the cannons, called the Wreck Raiders. Two others and I came to the spot with the "Ark" and confirmed the boys find - looking over the cannons ourselves. Then we asked that the club's barge be sent down and, while we were waiting for the barge, we talked with the boys. They agreed that the cannons should be put in a museum in Plattsburgh. We suggested our Naval Museum, as we have worked so hard in bringing it up to what it is today, and they agreed. Everything went fine at first. Cannons and anchor came up and we took them to the Marina - followed by the three boys in another boat. Meanwhile, the other diving club arrived on the scene and this is when the story started to change. Members of this other club (the Scuba Explorers) indicated to the boys and their mothers that they wore the white hats and we wore the black. When we loaded the cannons onto Frank Pabst's truck, the mothers said the cannons would not be available for public display in a museum but would instead be taken to their own lawns. The Wreck Raiders are not just a scuba diving group but through our diving, come into contact with history. We are very interested in history – especially the Naval aspects. Consequently, we refused to deliver the cannons to the Vernooy and Davidson front lawns. (Munn's mother was not involved in this confrontation.)"

Brandstetter further explained, "Frank Pabst had already contacted Dr. Allen Everest, historian at Plattsburgh State University, to tell him of the find and where the cannons would be taken for examination. We told the parents that Dr. Everest had been contacted and would examine the cannons at our museum, but they had those dollar signs in their eyes and insisted that the cannons be returned to their residences. During the stand off, Frank again called Dr. Everest and asked if he would accept the cannons for the state and "he heartily agreed."

Frank recalls, "Since the State University College had accepted the cannons I told Dr. Everest that I would hold them either in the back of my truck, or in our museum, for pickup by the college. Before the college came to get them, the Scuba Explorers brought a small truck down to the Marina, backed it up to my truck and proceeded to transfer the cannons from my truck to theirs. We knew that what they were doing wasn't right, but as ownership of the guns was in question, we made no attempt to stop them. The cannons were taken back to Cliff Haven and dumped on the lawns of the Vernooy and Davidson homes."

A front-page headline in the *Plattsburgh-Press Republican* the following day proclaimed, "Historic Underwater Find Exciting, Controversial." The by-line reported "Two 18th century cannons found Sunday at the bottom of Lake Champlain have created a flurry of excitement and some controversy. They have been described as the biggest discovery of this kind in the history of the North Country." (Thirty-one years later this find would be eclipsed by the finding and recovery of the anchor from the British warship Confiance) "They have attracted the interest of historians near and far…State Historian Dr. Louis Tucker was sent to Plattsburgh…on a fact-finding mission. College historians are pouring over books and archives in an effort to trace the origin of the two cannons, which were hauled into the sunlight Sunday after being hidden in 30 feet of water near Crab Island (This is in error, they were actually recovered quite close to the Cliff Haven shore in about 8-10 feet of water), for more than 200 years."

Frank recalls, "News of the discovery resulted in divers descending on the area like locusts to a field of beans. At first the State Police watched over the sight and shooed divers away, but after a short time they were called away and the divers were practically bumping into each other in their quest for booty that would turn into dollars. Although the paper would report the finding of 'two large anchors and a musket,' a hell-uva lot more artifacts were recovered and disappeared into Canada, or wherever."

In addition to the controversy over ownership or 'right of possession', a controversy arose over the origin and identity of the ship the cannons had been on. Dr. Everest of SUC at Plattsburgh theorized that the guns and anchor came from the *"Muskellunge"* a French vessel that sunk in the fall of 1759. He reported in the *Press-Republican,* "In the fall of 1759, Captain Loring had readied a small English fleet near Ticonderoga and Crown Point and headed north on Lake Champlain to clear the way for the English. He spotted Captain LaBar and his three French vessels near Crab Island late in the evening and planned a morning attack. But there was no battle. The French scuttled two of the vessels, ran the third ashore and left the area on land. The French vessels, like the *"Muskellunge"* were described by the French as 'xebec' or a large row galley with a sail rig." Dr. Everest came to this conclusion because he knew of no other vessels sunk in the vicinity. Forensic examination revealed "the cannons – both dated 1758 – were German made for King George II of England according to markings on the cannons which showed the name of the maker. A.S. Chalch was a noted gun maker employed by the village arsenal in England in the 18th century."

The question arose, "So, if the cannons were manufactured by a German for the English navy, how did they end up on a French ship? After identifying the manufacturer of the guns, Dr. Everest and Lake Champlain historian Oscar Bredenberg theorized that perhaps the cannons were from the British warship *"Finch"* which grounded on a reef near Crab Island during the War of 1812. However, if that were the case, the question then arose, as to how the heavy guns ended up nearly a mile away, near the shore of Cliff Haven? Eventually these experts concluded that the British had brought the *'La Masquinonge* to the surface with everything aboard, but the two cannon were not raised with the ship."

Subsequent investigation of the cannons origin during a prolonged court battle over their ownership revealed how the two British field cannon ended up on the French xebec *La Masquinonge*. According to a legal brief filed by the New York State Attorney General on December 11, 1984, "...They were cast in 1748 in Woolrich, England, and were designed as field pieces for the British Royal Artillery. The prominent insignia "GR" (Georgius Rex, Latin for King George) designates each 1000pound cannon as property of the Crown, and other markings establish the order in which they were cast and the name of the Master Founder at Woolrich. The British transported the cannon to North America for use in their struggle with the French for control of the New World. The North Country was a fervently contested battleground during this conflict, the French and Indian War. On August 9, 1757, the French captured the cannon on the shores of Lake George when forces led by the Sieur de Montcalm overran the British at Fort William Henry. The French conveyed their newly acquired weapons to Fort Carillon (Fort Ticonderoga) and mounted them aboard the French Xebec (small warship) *Muskellunge*, which was used by the French to protect Lake Champlain.

On October 12, 1759, the French scuttled the *Muskellunge* and two other boats as they withdrew from the advances of British troops led by General Jeffrey Amherst. Those items that could not be carried away were thrown overboard and the ships were then sunk in shallow water near the mainland, two miles south of Plattsburgh...Ironically, the British found and raised the ships, which became part of the

British fleet. The cannon, meanwhile, remained undiscovered" (Until September 21, 1968).

Although the cannons origin was in question at the time they were pulled from the lake bottom, it was immediately obvious that they were indeed a very important historic find. What their final disposition would be, however, remained in question.

Dr. Hugh Flick, Associate Commissioner of Cultural Education in the State Education Department added to the muck and mire of the ownership controversy. Dr. Flick reported, "Suppose a merchant vessel were sunk in Lake Champlain, would the state own it? Even though the state owns the bottom of the lake and artifacts found on state property, the answer to this question could be 'no.'"

It was pointed out to Flick, "When a similar discovery was made in Lake George several years ago, the State Attorney General proved that the vessel was government property."

Flick responded by first stating, "It's a cloudy area." Then he qualified his answer by saying, "I suppose it's clear enough. The informal decision rendered by the Attorney General in the Lake George case was the deciding factor with respect to state ownership." He added, "The Commissioner of General Services... has been requested to contact the State Police to dispatch divers to Lake Champlain this week, or the first of next week at the latest. State Police divers will work with divers from the State Education Department to make a good covering of the ship (if it's there) and area." He went on to say, "The state wanted to be fair with the people who found the cannons and there was no question about the cannons staying in the Plattsburgh area, although they could be loaded for display in other areas from time to time. There is a need for better legislation providing for a 'reasonable system of rewards' and stiff penalties for 'seizure' and stealing artifacts."

Commissioner of General Services General C.V.R. Schuyler reported to the *Plattsburgh-Press Republican*, "State officials aren't in a big rush to claim the two cannons. The cannons won't run away." Schuyler added, "The State Education Department is most interested in seeing that other items in the lake were not disturbed."

Frank shook his head topped by a thick thatch of gray hair displaying a look of disgust on a weathered but handsome face, without displacing one hair of the thick gray mane gracing it; as he reflected on the issue and, in true Captain Pabst form opined, "An example of bureaucracy at its finest. What should have been a simple process to preserve a segment of Lake Champlain history turned into a quagmire of procrastination, fueled by the ineptness and uncertainty of several omnipotent officials with fancy titles but no courage or guts. There was never any doubt or question in my mind that the cannons were the property of the state. I just thought they rightfully belonged on display in Plattsburgh and not exploited by fortune seekers. After the State Police, State University, State Historical Society, State Education, General Services, and agencies I have forgotten exist, got involved, the cannons initially were displayed on lawns and eventually hidden in the private garages of fortune seekers. I knew divers would descend on the area in droves, and it was my goal and the goal of the Wreck Raiders to go about the recovery process legitimately and ensure that every artifact found was documented and placed in our museum for display."

In this regard, the day following the cannons discovery, Frank traveled to Albany to obtain a permit designating the Wreck Raiders as the sole authority authorized to recover artifacts from the site where the cannons were found. He was told by the State Education Department that it would take three months for the permit to be processed. Frank returned to Plattsburgh empty handed. Frustratingly, he would explain to this author, "When I went down to Albany I expected to be referred to many doors that would be closed in my face, that's the story of my life in dealing with government, so I really wasn't surprised. I explained that by the time the permit process cleared, the dive area would be picked clean by voracious vultures and important historical relics might be lost forever. I might just as well have talked to a wall."

Frank added, "At the time the cannon incident surfaced, the Wreck Raiders was a large club of well-trained divers and I supervised the Clinton County Sheriffs Department Dive Team. We had a good thing going and the Wreck Raiders were devoted to recovering historical artifacts from Lake Champlain and getting them into museums where they could be enjoyed by one and all. As a matter of fact, when our club first formed, we named ourselves *The Lake Champlain Underwater Historical Research Club*. Everyone had difficulty remembering that long title so after a time – because we were diving on a lot of shipwrecks – we changed the club name to *The Wreck Raiders*. Our main mission was to go diving, drink beer, have a good time, and preserve history. Everything that we brought up ended up going into museums so that the public, and especially schoolchildren, could physically observe items that shaped this great lake's history. We recovered many relics from the area around Valcour Island. When the club first got started, we would go out with a pail and dive only wearing a mask and snorkel. Lying on the bottom in that area was a lot of ordnance from the Revolutionary War naval battle between Benedict Arnold and the British Navy, which was fought in Valcour Straight. We were able to fill the pail with shot in about fifteen minutes and what we brought up was turned over to museums. Our efforts to obtain recognition and obtain certification of our museum from the state were stonewalled at every turn. Then the state's botching of this cannon incident just totally destroyed any credibility the state had. Instead of sharing recovered relics with the public, divers wound up placing the items in closets, in attics, on their fireplace mantel or sold them to private individuals."

As time passed without any decision from the state as to what should be done with the cannons, politicians became embroiled in the controversy over their rightful ownership, perhaps triggered by an editorial that appeared in the *Plattsburgh-Press Republican* on October 1, 1968. The editorial urged, "The story of the two cannons found on the bottom of Lake Champlain between Cliff Haven and Crab Island gets more fascinating by the hour…the ownership of the guns is still somewhat in doubt. The state however insists that by law anything on the bottom of the lake belongs to it and it seems likely that this claim will stick. The point is that the finding of two cannons is a tremendously important historical event, and very valuable, too. Some estimates have run as high as $100,000, and this complicates things…the youths who found the cannons certainly deserve something from the state if it takes over, as seems highly probable. We'd hate to think that the state would come in, grab the cannons and just say thanks. In truth, the rich historical significance of the find could best be appreciated right here in the area. If the cannons are taken and exhibited in a museum in Albany, much of the impact will be lost. Experts should be brought in to look at the cannons and offer guidance and direction for preserving them and keeping them from harm. By all means, these cannons should get the proper care and not be left about on lawns where people can chip them, try to peck off souvenirs and mark them up…We urge the state to take steps to see that the cannons, other relics, and the ship itself if possible, remain here in the area where so much of the great early American history took place. Where else could be more fitting?"

New York Assemblyman Louis Wolfe jumped into the fray announcing via the *Plattsburgh-Press Republican*, and other media venues, that, "He plans to investigate the existing laws covering the discovery of artifacts on state land and will seek legislation to provide remuneration to the discoverers of such artifacts." Wolfe proclaimed, "It's an unfair law that the finders are not given a financial reward for their efforts. A provision for rewards would serve two purposes: first it would pay the finders for their work and, secondly, it would encourage people to report their discoveries to the state." He added, "Nobody knows how many hundreds of valuable items have been taken from the area of the cannon discovery."

Frank attests, "I am certain that many artifacts such as muskets, musket balls, coins, uniform buttons, etc. were scrounged from the dive site after the discovery of the cannons because there was a lack of control over the area and the identity of many of the divers and their club affiliations were not documented. A lot of stuff disappeared into Canada."

Assemblyman Wolfe indicated to the press that, "He had received a formal request from the Clinton County Historical Society asking that the cannons be left in Plattsburgh." He noted that he promised, "to work in the direction of establishing a museum here and in this regard had contacted the *State University, the New York State Historic Trust and the Historical Society* which was also thinking along these lines and there was discussion centering on establishment of a museum at the DAR building."

Frank snorted with disgust as he explained, "All of this rhetoric was needless phony-baloney, because at the time the *Wreck Raiders* had established a maritime museum on Miller Street, and despite the fact that hundreds of school kids were already touring our museum learning Lake Champlain history, we were not given recognition or consideration by politicians and bureaucrats."

The disposition of the cannons remained unresolved for many years as the right of ownership proceeded at a snail's pace through the courts.

Thirty seven years after the day of his historic swim, 51year old Patrick Munn sat in his parents Cliff Haven home and reflected on the long ago September Sunday of his youth. As his mind rewound to the exciting, unforgettable moment, his pale blue eyes displayed a dreamy look and the reflection ignited a broad smile. "That was a very long time ago," he began, "but finding those cannons was one of the most exciting things that has taken place in my life. Pete, Mike and I decided to go spear fishing that afternoon. We donned snorkel, mask and swim fins and went searching for fish just off the Cliff Haven shoreline. We often did this, but that day we swam out a little farther than usual. We were probably about a 100yards off shore. I was actually the first to see a cannon on the bottom, but mistook it for a log. Then later when Mike yelled that he had found a cannon on the bottom, I swam over to the spot and saw that it was what I had mistakenly thought was a log. We were very excited and started searching the vicinity. The water was kind of choppy that day, and it caused us to momentarily lose the location of the find on the bottom. While searching for that cannon, we found the second one, and right with it was a very large anchor. We marked the find by tying a weight belt to either the anchor or a cannon. I had been a junior member of the *Wreck Raiders* Dive Club, so I swam in to shore and called Frank Pabst. I told him what we had found and Frank said that we should stay with the find and he would send someone from the club down. I don't recall who came down, but whoever it was, after diving and confirming we had found items of historical interest, informed us that the cannons and anchor would become the property of the state and they belonged in a museum. We were just excited kids, having no idea about the law regarding salvage of lake artifacts, or right of ownership, and didn't give much thought to the value of our find. We were just thrilled to have made such an important discovery. Neither did we realize that our discovery would give us local celebratory status, but it did. At first, we enjoyed the attention and were delighted to repeat our story to everyone. I don't think any of us realized that our discovery would result in a lot of conflict and animosity that would go unresolved for many years."

Patrick's parents, Robert "Bob" Munn and Patricia "Pat" Munn, still reside in the home of Patrick's youth, overlooking the west shore of Lake Champlain. Bob and Pat settled in Cliff Haven after Air Force Lieutenant Colonel Bob Munn was transferred to Plattsburgh, and came to love the little community nestled alongside Lake Champlain. Cliff Haven proved the perfect 'haven' to raise their 11 children, and the couple remained in their comfortable home after Bob's retirement from the military. Bob and Pat invited me into their home, introduced me to their son, Patrick, and treated my wife and me to hours of delightful conversation.

Bob Munn provided his own recollection of the events connected with the discovery of the cannons, "We were all naturally excited by the boys' discovery and the news quickly spread throughout Cliff Haven. A small crowd soon gathered on our lawn at lakeside to watch the recovery operation. While Frank Pabst's divers were working to raise the cannons, members of another dive group showed up. It was soon apparent that these fellows were in competition with the *Wreck Raiders*, because they told us that the cannons and anchor were worth a lot of money and we should hold onto them and not let the *Wreck Raiders* take them to their museum. Someone indicated that the cannons might be worth as much as $100,000. My son, once a member of the *Wreck Raiders*, told us that the artifacts belonged to the state, and I agreed that the artifacts belonged in a museum. After hearing that the boys' find was worth a lot of money, Michael and Peter's parents wanted to keep possession of the artifacts until their sons received reward for the recovery. After the cannons and anchor were retrieved from the lake bottom they, were taken to Pabst's marina by the *Wreck Raiders*. The next thing we knew they reappeared in Cliff Haven and were unloaded on the Vernooy and Davidson lawns. Peter and Michael's parents told us that they were going to hold onto them until the boy's received just compensation. I was of the opinion that no matter the value of the artifacts, they belonged in a museum and not on someone's lawn, so I didn't join in the cause. The day following the initial discovery, a swarm of divers descended on the site, and I am reasonably sure more artifacts were found, but I don't know exactly what they were or where they were taken. As a matter of fact, for the rest of that fall and throughout the following spring, summer and fall seasons, hordes of divers dove on the spot. I don't know who these divers were and I wonder if anyone from any agency of authority has any idea who they were, where they were from, or what they took out of the lake. The cannon remained in the possession of the Vernooy's and Davidson's for several years, before the state finally got around to taking them. Incredibly, they never bothered to take the anchor, and that is presently out on the back lawn of the Vernooy home, which is now under new ownership."

Pat added, "I think nearly 18 years passed before the state finally took possession of the cannons. I was never offered any compensation by the state and don't know if Mike and Peter received any. That is of little consequence to me because I am glad that they are finally mounted where they will be preserved and people can enjoy their history. I believe one of the cannons is presently on display up at Clinton County Community College, and the other is on display down in Crown Point."

Patrick was correct. One cannon is on display at Clinton County Community College, located on a bluff just south of Cliff Haven, and the other is on display in the Visitor's Center at Crown Point State Historical site, located at the south end of Lake Champlain. A swivel gun, anchors, muskets and a partial sword, which were also recovered from the Cliff Haven dive site, are on display at the Clinton County Historical Association Museum located at 48 Court Street, Plattsburgh, New York.

Historic Cannons

Helen Allen, a former director of the Clinton County Historical Association was contacted and recalled, "There was a great deal of controversy concerning the cannons recovered at Cliff Haven, and, naturally the Historical Association took an active interest. In 1982, the cannons were offered for sale in an auction brochure, and this caused great concern. We realized that if the cannons were sold, they could very well disappear into Canada or some other far away place. The association obtained the services of a local attorney who filed an Article 78, forcing the state to take action to recover those artifacts."

Mrs. Allen was surprised to learn that the large anchor found with the cannons had not been taken by the state and is still on the lawn of a residence in Cliff Haven.

According to a legal brief filed by the State Attorney General's Office, "In March of 1982, Vernooy and Davidson entered into a consignment agreement with Sotheby's to offer the cannon for public auction…Sotheby's proceeded to advertise the planned auction of the cannon, which had since been transferred to their New York County offices. Their publication, "Antiques," contained a photograph of the cannon and stated that the auction would take place on May 21 or May 22. News of the proposed auction shocked and dismayed State officials. The Director of the State Museum at the time believed that the sale of the cannon would not only violate the Education Law, but would also create the risk that an important part of the heritage of the State would be forever taken away from the people…On May 3, 1982, the Assistant Attorney General assigned to the matter, wrote a letter to Sotheby's, confirming a conversation that day, in which the state claimed title to the cannon and would assert its right to possession. Although Sotheby's initially agreed to withhold any auction of the cannon until the competing claims were resolved, it soon reversed its position. At the behest of consignors Vernooy and Davidson, the cannon were to be sold at auction subject to amended conditions of sale. These conditions of sale provided that Sotheby's would acknowledge the highest bidder(s) as having made an offer of purchase, and that such offer cannot be withdrawn or modified for a period of two years. The offer of purchase would be deemed withdrawn if it were determined that title to the cannon lies with the State."

The legal brief further noted, "John H.G. Pell, on behalf of the Fort Ticonderoga Association, offered the highest bids for the two cannon of $32,000 and $36,000, respectively, plus a 10% commission to Sotheby's for a total offering price of $74,800. Mr. Pell, who is a publisher of several historical works, and a well-known collector of historical artifacts, recognized the State's title to the cannon…"

The ongoing court action caught the attention of the *New York Post*, which ran an article titled *"2 Ancient Cannon Fodder for Lawyers"* in its May 27, 1982 edition "THE STATE has rolled out its big legal guns in an all-out campaign to recapture a couple of ancient cannon from two upstaters who fished them out of a lake while scuba diving. The rare bronze half-ton cannon – traced to the time of King George II – have embroiled rival historical groups up in Plattsburgh, where two teenagers found the guns in Lake Champlain in 1968…Manhattan Supreme Court Justice Bernard Nadel yesterday barred Sotheby from removing the cannon from the state pending further legal action. The court order was obtained by State Education Commissioner Gordon Ambach, who says the weapons were state property ever since Michael Davidson and Peter Vernooy found them. Ambach claims any object of archeological interest found in a lake belongs to the state. Davidson says the state should have come around 14 years ago. He and Vernooy consigned them for auction…'I deny that the cannon were improperly taken', Davidson, now 29, of Fort Lauderdale, Fla., said in court papers. His lawyer, William O'Donnell, said that the state has waived its right, if any, to possess the cannon by waiting 14 years to try to enforce its belated and long-delayed claim. Zwickel (Assistant Attorney General) said that the people of this state should not be deprived of their right to view the cannon…"

The Vernooy's and Davidson's eventually moved out of Cliff Haven and Peter Vernooy found employment in a career, which required his relocation to another part of New York State. The now retired 50year old was contacted via telephone and provided details that solved the mystery as to why it took 18 years for the state to place his historic find on public display.

Peter related, "Although the cannons had been on the bottom of Lake Champlain for over two-hundred years, they were in excellent condition. Pat called Frank Pabst to raise the cannons from the lake bottom, and Frank told us that the law provided that the guns belonged to the state. We all agreed that we wanted the cannons to end up in a museum, but we also recognized our find could be worth a great deal of money. My parents contacted their attorney, Charles Lewis, and he recommended we retain possession of them until the law was researched and the cannons appraised. So my parents and Mike's parents insisted that the cannons be taken to our homes until those facts were determined. We learned that the recovery of artifacts from the waters in New York State fell under the purview of Section 233 of the State Education Law. The law provided that artifacts found above or below the 'water' were considered the property of New York State. Specific bodies of water were named and designated in the law and, for some reason, Lake Champlain was not included, probably because Lake Champlain is bounded by Vermont, New York and Canada, and was deemed international waters. Pabst and his divers recovered the cannon from the lake bottom, and when they were on his barge, they took them down to the Peru dock at Frank's marina. It had taken several hours to recover the guns and it was getting along in the evening by the time they reached the dock. As it was late, it was decided to leave the cannons on board the barge overnight. Each cannon was 1120 pounds of solid bronze and both were precariously balanced on board the small barge. When Frank or one of his diver's stepped onto the end of the deck where the cannon were lying, the barge flipped up and dropped both guns back into the lake. The following morning, at 8 a.m., they were again pulled out of the water. We were at the dock with a pickup truck and directed the cannons be loaded into the truck. Then they were driven up to Cliff Haven and unloaded on my front lawn. Our intent was that the state eventually take control of the guns and display them in a museum, but we wanted compensation and recognition for finding them, and figured possession was nine-tenths of the law. Shortly after the cannon were placed on my lawn, a state police car pulled into our driveway and two troopers came to our door. They informed my parents and me that they were there to take possession of 'state property.' We asked them to show us documentation proving that the cannons were state property, and of course, they had none. After that, around the clock, a state police car occupied by two troopers was parked on the street in front of our house and they watched the cannons that were out on our front lawn. After about two weeks, they abandoned their surveillance. As winter approached we transferred the cannons from our lawn into our garage. We did this for about 9 years, all the while waiting for the state to take some sort of action, but 'they' seemed disinterested. We would learn through our attorney that Attorney General Louis Lefkowitz had submitted a memorandum to the Chancellor of State Education, advising him to 'walk softly in the area of claiming the cannons.' When I was in my late 20's, Mike and I decided to contact somebody to have the cannons appraised. We contacted Christy's & Sotheby's Auction Houses and ended up being visited by a representative from the New York City office of Sotheby's. This fellow examined the cannons and told us that the guns were quite valuable, but to command the highest price, they should be put on display in a gallery where people would see them and make an offer. The appraiser told us that the pair would probably be worth about $100,000. So we contracted with Coolidge Movers of Plattsburgh to take the cannons to Sotheby's New York City office. Sotheby's photographed them and then put the photos on display in their worldwide catalogue. The director of the Clinton County Historical Association (Helen Allen) apparently saw the advertisement in the Sotheby catalogue and called – or had an attorney – call the Attorney General's office. The Attorney General slapped an injunction on Sotheby's forbidding the sale of the cannons until their ownership was determined by a court of law. As I recall, this was in 1981, and the action commenced a long legal battle. Mike and I ended up making several trips to court in Manhattan, where the issue was being decided. After 3 or 4 years of legal wrangling, the matter wound up in the New York State Appellate Court, which referred the final resolution back to the Court of Claims, with their ruling that basically said, 'The cannons should not leave the possession of the public, so the state should take possession of them; however, Mike and I should be adequately compensated. The Court of Claims awarded Mike and me a sum of money that reimbursed our legal fees and an additional sum for keeping the cannons in our care and custody'."

Peter concluded his reflection on the past with a touch of irony. "You know if the state of New York had sat down with us and negotiated in a reasonable manner, they could have taken possession of the guns shortly after we found them, and they weren't even interested in the anchor. We mentioned that we had a large anchor that came up with the cannons and the state's response was, 'old anchors are a dime a dozen and we aren't interested in it'."

On March 2, 1984, the New York State Supreme Court ruled that the State of New York was entitled to take immediate possession of the cannons and ordered that the matter of compensation to Vernooy and Davidson be assigned to the Court of Claims. The exact wording of the compensation being, "reasonable salvage and all necessary expenses incurred in the preservation and keeping of the property pursuant to Navigation Law, section 132…"

The matter of compensation would go unresolved for another two years, and eventually in 1986, the Court of Claims awarded Vernooy and Davidson reimbursement for legal expenses and an additional sum for preservation of the cannons, thus closing out an 18 year legal battle and controversy that still ignites varied sentiments in the Cliff Haven and Plattsburgh communities.

The state took possession of the cannon in 1984 and submitted them to an artifacts restoration facility for treatment with a preservative before placing them on display.

Peter Vernooy voiced his displeasure with the treatment stating, "When we found the cannons they were in excellent condition and, as they were bronze, after being exposed to the air, they both took on a natural light green patina. After the state took possession of them, some sort of preservative was applied that turned them a brown color. The color makes them appear fake, and diminishes their historic value."

Frank concludes telling this chapter of his life in classic euphemistic style, "The *Wreck Raiders* put in nearly 60 dive hours on this misadventure, which cost us a hell-uva lot of money. All we got out of it was sweat, aggravation, grief, and a kick in the ass by bureaucrats more concerned about political appeasement than enforcing the law. If the bureaucrats and politicians had truly cared about the preservation of Lake Champlain history, as they proclaimed, why did it take them 18 years to pick up the cannon, and why did they leave the anchor that we recovered? Today, it is gathering rust on the lawn of a private citizen! That anchor belongs in a museum."

The Juniper

Losing employment at WPTZ was a blow to the Pabst family; however, it was only another minor set back in a life of setbacks for the ever-ambitious entrepreneur. Having now reached middle age, Frank had achieved the distinction of having worked at more jobs than anyone else he knew. 'Til this still young state of life, he had worked as a: crew-member on a tugboat, newspaper boy, underwater diver, moving van driver, tractor-trailer driver, junkyard owner, New York City taxi driver, tow truck operator, Army supply sergeant, Army photographer, auto-dealer employee, driver of a U.S. mail truck, steeple jack, underwater diving instructor, marina operator, ice cream delivery man, bread truck diver, television personality, disc jockey, television sales, television switcher, marine salvage operator, museum curator (of sorts) and supervisor of a Sheriff's department boat patrol on Lake Champlain. As previously stated, Frank's dream and goal was to become owner of his own business and, having fallen in love with Lake Champlain, he recognized that the majestic, beautiful body of water provided the means to fulfill that life dream. Each year the lake attracted thousands of sailors, power boaters, fishermen, divers, tourists and thrill seekers hoping to catch a glimpse and even better, photograph, of "Champ," the shy and elusive creature of the lake.

A previous chapter portrayed Frank's early business ventures on the lake, which Frank describes as, "I enjoyed every one of them, but unfortunately I couldn't feed my family on fun. Although having fun and enjoying life is important, ever mounting bills and the inability to pay them, motivated me to keep searching for a more profitable enterprise."

For some time Frank envisioned owning and operating a tour boat on Lake Champlain, but lacked the funds needed to bring this dream to fruition.

Frank's seemingly always-smiling blue eyes, display a special sort of nostalgic charm as he reflects on the fulfillment of finally achieving ownership of a tour boat and setting sail (in a manner of speaking) as *"Heritage Adventures, Inc."* At last he had found his true niche in life and in the process embarked on a 25-year voyage that would establish "Captain Frank" as a living legend of Lake Champlain.

Captain Frank's face glows with pride whenever he tells the story of launching his career as a tour boat operator. "I tried a couple of times to get a tour boat up and running. My first try was a tour to Schuyler Island, using a small boat, and my second was with a 40-foot steel tug, named *'Morning Star.'* I couldn't get Coast Guard certification for either, so gave up. However, the desire to operate a tour boat remained in my mind, and I was continually mulling over ways to bring this dream to reality. Although there were a few small tour boat operations on the lake, there weren't any operating out of Plattsburgh and none that I can recall that provided passengers the story of the important role Lake Champlain played in the shaping of America. I dreamed of operating that sort of tour boat out of Plattsburgh and kept telling myself – someday. That someday came in 1976 when I learned that Bill Scott, owner of Scott Rigging Company in Burlington, Vermont, wanted to sell his boat. I was familiar with *'The Juniper'* and had been eyeing her for some time. The rugged 63.5-foot, steel-hulled boat had a 30-foot beam and 7.5-foot draft. Her displacement was 85 tons. She was powered by powerful diesel engines, and had twin screws. She was old, but she was sturdy and I knew she would serve well for the idea I had in mind. *The Juniper* had faithfully plied the waters of the Hudson River, East River and Lake Champlain for 32 years when I put my bid in for her, and she had a rather interesting history. A product of the Yonkers boat yard she was built in 1945 for the Pepsi-Cola Bottling Company, for the purpose of hauling cases of soft drink up and down the Hudson and East Rivers. This use was necessitated because World War II resulted in a scarcity of trucks for private industry."

Frank produced before and after photographs of the ship before continuing and laughed as he pointed to an original photo of what the ship looked like in its early years. "This sturdy lady plying the waters in the vicinity of New York City during the late forties as a floating soft drink vendor, was then named the *"Big Bottle."* Other than a small pilothouse, the entire deck surrounded by a four foot steel rail was completely open. She transported a lot of Pepsi for a couple of years and then in 1947, the availability of delivery trucks made The *Big Bottle* obsolete. She was tied to a pier in Astoria, Queens and was sort of neglected for about five years. I first saw the *Big Bottle* as a lad working on the tugs. She was tied up at the Pepsi Cola pier, and even at that young age there was something about the unattractive, stout vessel that caught my eye.

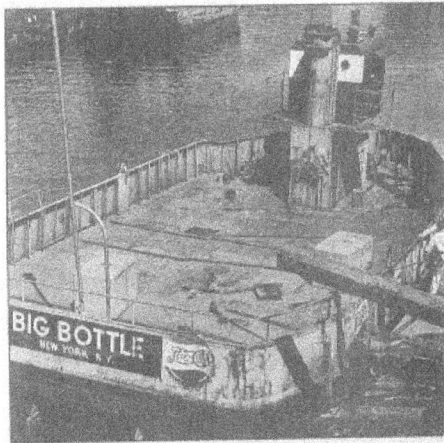

SUNDAY, JULY 23, 1995   PAGE D-3

irough 50 years

Photo Provided

notes. "We installed three miles of underwater cable for New York Telephone and removed an old oil dolphin, a manmade island that oil barges tied up to in the bay near Westport."

The vessel has made many local residents happy when raising funds for charitable organizations. "We have donated the boat to help raise funds for the Riverwalk Project, Beekman-town school kids who had to replace their school-trip money, the soup kitchen at the Episcopal Church and many other

benevolent activities," Pabst said. "We believe in the local community and being part of it. We hire many local kids, too. Sometimes it's their first job."

Short-range plans for the 50th birthday celebration are to hold some special events at the end of the month. But what about the next 50 years?

"Someone younger will be involved with this boat then, I hope," Pabst said. "I need to have some leisure time. It's been 19 years, 18 hours a day from Memorial Day to September and I'm getting a little tired."

Big Bottle

Staff Photo/Mike Dowd

At right, the Juniper is shown in its early days as a freight carrier while, above, its present duties as a Lake Champlain tour boat are shown.

The Juniper Tourboat

In 1952, the Lake Champlain Ferry Company bought the *Big Bottle* and put her in service as a ferry on the lake. Getting the boat to Lake Champlain proved a challenge and is quite interesting as well. Although the crew removed all the extras off the wheelhouse, the boat still could not pass under several bridges. So the crew dumped 15 tons of gravel on the deck to lower the boat in the water, then doors to the crew quarters and engine room were cut in half and the lower parts of the boat welded shut. She scraped the sides of the canal locks a little but eventually made it into Lake Champlain. The ferry company renamed her *The Juniper* after an island located just outside Burlington, Vermont. For the next 15-years, *The Juniper* ferried cars back and forth across the lake from Essex, New York to Charlotte, Vermont.

In 1967 William (Bill) Scott, a rigger and crane operator from Burlington, bought the *Juniper*, mounted a motor home on the aft deck and turned her into his personal yacht. Bill and I were a lot alike when it comes to starting up new business. The yacht served him well for a time, but it was sort of expensive to maintain, and it suddenly came to him that he could make money with the *Juniper*. He outfitted the boat with 'pushing knees' (steel grid work welded on the bow) and went into the marine-contracting business. When Bill began using the *Juniper* for business, he purchased a fine yacht to cruise the lake for pleasure."

This reflection evoked a chuckle and Frank momentarily digressed from the story of the Juniper to relate the story of what happened to Scott's yacht, while at the same time eulogizing his friend. "Bill was out sailing one night and left a port hole open on the yacht. The yacht began taking on water through the port and it sank off Juniper Island. Bill survived that incident, was paid for the loss of his yacht by the insurance company and promptly went out and purchased another yacht.

As you can guess, Bill loved Lake Champlain nearly as much as I, and because of our mutual love for this lake and competition in marine salvage, we became acquainted. Bill was a hard working fellow and deserved to enjoy every moment he could on the lake. Unfortunately, he died in the cab of his crane while driving down a hill in Montpelier, Vermont. He was about 65 when he died. Bill was quite a man. He taught me a lot about doing business on the lake. He was also one of the riggers who helped bring the *Ticonderoga* up across the swamp for placement in the Shelburne museum which was no easy feat."

Pausing for a moment, Frank lifted a gnarled hand to his face, rubbed his eyes then returned to the telling of how he purchased the *Juniper*. "Anyway, using the *Juniper* in his marine salvage business worked out for a while and then in 1971, Bill retired the *Juniper* and put her up for sale. I examined every inch of the old vessel and found that, despite her age, she was in excellent condition. I saw that with some revisions to her superstructure, she could be converted into a passenger cruise vessel and I longed to own her. I also recognized that her solid construction, and powerful diesel engines would enable her to perform double duty as a tour boat and marine salvage vessel. I wanted the *Juniper* real bad. The problem was, I didn't have two-nickels to rub together and didn't have sufficient capital to float a loan, but of course, Bill didn't know that. I went over to Burlington and wrote Bill a check for $5000 on an account that had about $500 in it. That was on a Friday. Then I returned to Plattsburgh and wrote up a prospectus outlining a business plan, and then immediately distributed the prospectus to potential investors. My wife and family pitched in and we started making calls to potential business partners. By Monday I had sold $8000 in stock on a boat I didn't own, in a company that didn't exist. What those intrepid investors bought into was an idea. While we were scampering to come up with the funds needed to finalize purchase of the *Juniper*, Scott contacted the Lake Champlain Ferry Company to see if they were interested in buying the *Juniper*. Bill called me and related the news that the ferry company offered to pay him $7000 more than I was paying for the boat. At first I thought it was a ruse to finagle more money out of me, but later I learned that the ferry company didn't want me to have the *Juniper*, so they offered Bill more money. As I already had a contract of sale with him, I told him that he couldn't back out of our deal. Bill was adamant and said that he had to have more money. At the time I had a scuba shop and one of the guys in our scuba club was a pilot. He owned a little twin-engine Aztec. I had flown with him from time to time just to get a ride in the airplane. I asked him to play a little charade for me and he agreed. By this time, I could write Scott another check for $5000 and my flier friend agreed to fly over to Burlington and deliver the payment to Bill. I called Bill back and told him that 'my' pilot would be at the Burlington airport with another payment. That evening, my pilot friend flew over to Burlington carrying my check. Scott was waiting for him. After landing, my pilot friend looking quite elegant in a leather jacket with white scarf tucked in the collar walked up to Bill, handed him the check, looked him in the eye and said, 'Look, you don't know who you are messing with. Here's your check, and it would be wise to get off Mr. Pabst's back.' Well, Bill did get off my back and as a matter-of-fact he even helped me out, when the old hierarchy from the ferry company tried to screw me. I took possession of the *Juniper* and brought her over to Plattsburgh on April 22, 1976. A group of my divers accompanied me to Burlington to help get the *Juniper* rigged for the trip to Plattsburgh. I hadn't operated a boat the size of the *Juniper* for 20 years so I had mixed emotions of elation and anxiety. As it turned out, the *Juniper* was as eager to get back into action as I was to put her in action, and she responded magnificently. Although resembling a tugboat and designed for hauling freight and performing as a workhorse on the water, her stout body belied quality, grace and beauty that rivaled sleek-looking cruise ships. During that maiden voyage across the lake from Burlington to Plattsburgh, I fell in love with the stout old lady, and my wife didn't mind this rival for her affection, because she came to love her too.

In my haste to get a lake cruise up and running, I had overlooked a couple of major details. At the time, I was operating my marine business from shoreline property owned by the railroad. I had helped the railroad out a couple of times down in the Westport and Port Kent area, and didn't charge them much. In return, I had been given permission to use their yard located next to the Plattsburgh Boat Basin to launch from. If I were to operate a tour boat from that location, I needed a lease agreement with the railroad to ensure I wasn't suddenly dispossessed at some point down the line. The second problem was that we didn't have a dock in place to berth a boat the size of the *Juniper* and which would permit easy boarding of passengers. I started scrambling. Many times in my life I managed to put the cart before the horse but must have had some sort of divine providence watching over me, because I always managed to come up with a horse."

This self-directed criticism using a common cliché evoked a laugh as Frank reflected on how he managed to acquire control of the valuable chunk of lakeside real estate. He continued, "It wasn't that I hadn't tried to obtain a lease. I had called the railroad company office several times, trying to speak with someone in their real estate department about obtaining a lease, but was always told, 'someone will get back to you.' No one did get back to me and now here I was about to start up a business from property that I was on as a guest. I had heard of Mr. Stertzing, the 'big shot' at D & H railroad because of a controversy that occurred over removal of an old wooden trestle that crossed the Saranac River in front of the McDonough monument. He had his railroad workers come into Plattsburgh, demolish the trestle and replace it with a steel one, without notifying the city or receiving the city's blessing to tie up local traffic. There was some ballyhoo about it, but Stertzing responded by saying the bridge belonged to the railroad, and the City of Plattsburgh didn't have anything to say about its removal and replacement. I called the railroad's corporate office, identified myself as 'Mr. Pabst' and it was assumed that I was the Pabst beer baron, whom I didn't know, and had never met. I got through to Mr. Stertzing, and explained that I needed a lease agreement from the railroad for operation of my business from the railroad's lakeside property in Plattsburgh."

Mr. Stertzing put me in immediate contact with his real estate department and they drew up a lease agreement.

My little spot of operation on the lake in the confines of a railroad yard didn't look like much, but it was actually steeped in history. There was a large warehouse adjacent to the shoreline and at one time a large pier at the shoreline permitted lake steamers to tie up and unload coal that would be moved into the warehouse. This coal was subsequently used to fuel the furnaces that powered railroad steam engines. Of course that was in a bygone era and at the time I secured my lease, the warehouse was being used by the *Plattsburgh-Press Republican* to store rolls of paper for newsprint. In 1893, the pier served as the Plattsburgh terminal for arriving and departing passengers traveling on the steamboat *Ticonderoga*.

Having cleared the hurdle of obtaining control of a small chunk of property that didn't look like much but, which in truth, was a piece of prime lakefront real estate, I commenced construction of a dock. All of my capital – and then some – was tied up in the *Juniper*, so I had to figure out a way of glomming on to the material needed for this project. I wanted a dock that would survive the rigors of climate change and destruction by winter ice. I 'obtained' pieces of railroad track from the railroad and used them as pilings. Then we went back 20 feet into the land and welded on a horizontal stringer, attaching a 3foot plate to it. That was my tie back for the dock, so that when the pressure came in, it came against the steel plate that was well buried. I had determined that this type of construction would better serve our operation than trying to operate from a shore dock, which had a fulcrum effect and was subjected to the movement of waves. Our dock was well constructed. We back filled it with stone, put a mesh on top, then backfilled over the mesh with gravel. Then we capped it off with blacktop. As usual, my dive buddies and group of stalwart friends pitched in to help with the construction. We had just started work when a representative from New York State's Department of Environmental Conservation showed up. I immediately recognized his appearance was not for the purpose of commending us for improving the esthetic quality of Lake Champlain."

"What are you doing?" the stern faced DEC inspector asked.

"I'm making improvements to an already existing structure. I responded, displaying my very best smile. I was familiar with DEC regulations dealing with Lake Champlain and knew that improvements could be made to an already existing structure without seeking approval from the DEC. Fortunately this area was located well out of the geographic confines additionally controlled by the Adirondack

Park Commission, because dealing with that entity is a whole new nightmare."

The DEC inspector put his hands on his hips gazed intently into the water lapping the shoreline and responded, "What existing structure?"

"I pointed to the surface of the water and answered, down there are the remains of pilings from the dock that once was here. I am making improvements to that dock. Of course, I said this with a straight face while displaying a smile of elfin sincerity. My charm sometimes proves lucky, and fortunately, I was in luck that day."

"Look," the DEC Inspector replied, "I can either write you a citation or issue you a permit authorizing construction. You can consider this your lucky day!"

"He issued me a permit on the spot, thereby saving me from having to jump through a myriad of bureaucratic hoops, which would have taken a lot of time and probably a lot of money.

When we arrived in Plattsburgh, I pulled the *Juniper* into the cove and we tied her up to a large tree. That tree still bears the scars of the damage inflicted on it by the *Juniper's* rubbing against it. I will never forget that day. After going ashore, we (diving club and investors in the business) took stock of our investment and popped a keg of beer to celebrate. Of course before commencing tours on the lake, the *Juniper* required some revisions. Basically, we needed to re-design the grand old workboat and convert her into a passenger vessel. We also needed to pass a Coast Guard inspection for approval as a passenger vessel. I had been told that the *Juniper* had been inspected by the Coast Guard once before and passed with flying colors; getting the Coast Guard to approve her for operation as a tour boat would be easy and how naïve an assumption that proved to be! I contacted the Coast Guard to arrange for inspection and was told that the inspection required the *Juniper* being taken out of the water for a complete going over to test the strength and stability of the bottom from bow to stern. The only outfit on the lake large enough to transport the *Juniper* out of water was the Champlain Ferry Company, and the owners didn't care for me because they saw me as competition. They wanted to buy the *Juniper* so as to eliminate a perceived threat to their business. I contacted the Ferry Company and was told that they wouldn't haul me. We faced a dilemma. If the ferry company wouldn't haul the *Juniper,* then I couldn't get her inspected, and if I didn't pass inspection, I couldn't get into business. There was an exchange of calls with the owners of the Ferry Company who treated me with arrogance and condescension. I was ordered – not asked – to be in the ferry company office at 8 in the morning, on a specific day, to discuss business arrangements. I wasn't going to be cowed by them, so I responded, 'If you want to see me, you come over to my office.' At the time, my office was a little camp trailer set up in 'the cove.' The owners of the ferry company came over (from Vermont) to my office and they arrived full of pomp and circumstance. They informed me of the existence of a covenant in the *Juniper's* title, which precluded use of the *Juniper* for transportation purposes on Lake Champlain. I responded, 'Look, I'm not going to be hauling horses, pigs and cattle across the lake. I'm going to be taking people from point A and returning them to point A, and doing a historic tour around the islands. So if you want to argue with the two judges and the lawyers that have shares in this corporation, you're going to have to try it over here in Clinton County, and right now they are very happy to have a tour boat operating here in town. I don't think your chances of winning would be good. My words made them sizzle like a drop of water on a hot griddle, but they finally saw wisdom in what I told them and they did not pursue any legal action concerning the covenant. They did try to frustrate our getting started though – probably hoping a long delay would break my already broke bank account. I was told that they couldn't haul the Juniper for inspection until October. The Coast Guard inspection requirement was that the Juniper be taken out of the water for inspection. I pondered how to do this for a while, then gave Bill Scott a call and asked if he could help out. Bill came over to Plattsburgh, bringing a 100-ton crane. We put two cables under the *Juniper*, hoisted her up with the crane, and rolled her onto her side. The guys in my diving club pitched in and we wire brushed the bottom. Their payment was a barrel of beer and some hot dogs. When we had the bottom clean, I called the Coast Guard, informed them that I had the *Juniper* out of the water and they agreed to come over to perform the inspection. The Commander of the Coast Guard installation at Burlington – Lieutenant Steve McCall, a fine young man – personally performed the inspection. Steve would go on to become the Commander of the Valdez Coast Guard unit and was there when Joe Hazelwood ran the *Exxon Valdez* aground.

Steve climbed into a skiff and went under the *Juniper* with a chipping hammer. He tested the strength of the hull, inspected the engine room, checked my valves, did a stability test and gave the *Juniper* his seal of approval. To satisfy the stability test, we loaded 16000 pounds of miscellaneous material – barrels filled with water, counterweights from cranes, etc. – on board and rolled all that stuff from side to side. We were finally certified to commence our tour boat operation, but we needed to perform some renovations before putting the *Juniper* in service. For one thing, we needed to put a roof on the boat. I checked with Vermont Structural Steel, and they wanted $20,000 to put a roof on it. Fortunately, I had a lot of good friends who made their living in various trades. Three of them - Earl Black, Walt Blayhut and Dale Lockhart - were welders. I explained the need for a roof on the *Juniper* and without hesitation, these fine gentlemen agreed to help out. We bought the steel and instead of just setting the beams on top of the steel, we used 'I beams,' notched them, notched the pipes connecting to them, and fitted them together before welding the seams. The result was I had 20-inches of welded surface on every joist supporting the roof. All it cost me for this excellent work was the price of the steel, some beer and a few steaks.

I've always been blessed with friends who enjoyed the fun things that I did and willingly pitched in when there was work to do. Their reward usually consisted of free flowing beer, a few hot dogs, an occasional steak and a lot of laughter because our work sessions were fun and the lake was therapy from their daily rigors of life. Mostly, they were guys from my diving club – Tom Tucker, Randy Larkin, Walt Blayhut, etc. - who had great love and affection for Lake Champlain.

I designed the roof with the intention of being able to box the girders and put a second deck on the boat once the business turned a profit. That proved to be sort of an illusion of grandeur that never came to fruition.

By the time we had everything ready to start operation, I was flat broke. What little surplus money we had been able to scrounge up was spent on material required on the boat such as life jackets, chairs, fire extinguishers, etc. There wasn't any money left for advertising and so my investors starting spreading the word that Plattsburgh was about to have its very own tour boat. We embarked our first passengers and set sail on our maiden voyage June 24, 1976, without a great deal of fanfare and little celebration. Of course, 1976 marked the bicentennial of the American Revolution, and with all the local history connected with that magnanimous event, I anticipated having a very profitable year. Those expectations were dashed because the talk of terrorism and problems at the Olympics which caused many people to celebrate the bicentennial at home. We wound up the season $40,000 in the red. Still, I am an eternal optimist and I had a gut feeling that business was about to improve and we would turn a profit.

The first part of the season we stretched a truck tarp across the steel spider works. If it looked like rain, crewmen would climb up, walk the spider work, unroll the tarp and tie it down. Unless we were charted for a special party or event, each lake cruise consisted of about a two-hour slow tour south, around Valcour Island, the backside of Crab Island, then back to the dock. Occasionally we reversed the tour and passed behind Crab Island first. Either route treated passengers to one of the most scenically beautiful and historic important portions of the lake. We had mounted speakers on the Juniper's superstructure, which allowed everyone on board to hear safety instructions and announcements, and listen to my narrated story of the magnificent historical events that took place on the very stretch of water being traversed. I recorded a canned narration that could be played, but most often gave it to them live. Passengers were regaled with historic fact, and lake-lore stories, many of which were about 'Champ,' the shy reptilian prehistoric creature that calls the lake home. We cruised slowly past Crab Island, and while doing so, I told the exciting history of the desolate-looking environment inhabited only by a magnificent pointed obelisk – similar to the Washington monument but, of course, on a much smaller scale – erected to commemorate and honor the role the island played as a field hospital during the War of 1812. I provided a synopsis of the naval battle fought in Cumberland Bay in 1814, resulting in capitulation by the British, and how important this victory was in establishing the fledgling United States of America as a super power. I told the story of the naval battle between American and British ships that occurred in Valcour Straight during 1776. Various Plattsburgh Air Base areas of importance were pointed out as we cruised slowly past them. The community of Cliff Haven was pointed out as the location of the former Catholic Summer School, which was associated with Rutgers University providing students and scholars a place to enjoy a summer vacation while continuing their education. I directed their attention to the area at Cliff Haven where three teenagers discovered two cannons from a French ship that sunk in 1759, and I took pleasure in describing the role I played in the cannons' salvage from the bottom. Clinton County Community College, a prominent landmark on the lake, located on the bluff at Woodcliff, was pointed out and the details of how the once elegant Champlain Hotel, visited by world dignitaries, evolved into a present day college campus. As we cruised by the beautiful Valcour lighthouse I told the story of its origin and provided some anecdotal tidbits of information from its years of operation. As we cruised around the south end of Valcour, I pointed out Garden Island, also known as Gunboat Island, and told the story of how a French pay ship loaded down with a payroll of gold, struck a reef connected to the island, became stuck on the reef, and over the course of a harsh winter, was disintegrated by ice. A story associated with the battle of Valcour Straight, explains how Garden Island came to be referred to as Gunboat Island. It seems that when the British discovered that Benedict Arnold and his ships had somehow slipped past them during the night, lookouts searching the early morning mist reported seeing the outline of an American gunboat. The British wasted a lot of munitions and time, firing at the outline, which, when the mist cleared, proved to be Garden Island. *Juniper* passengers marveled at this story and were wide-eyed with awe when we cruised past the island and I told them about the French ship and that its cargo of gold have not been discovered to this day. As we cruised along the east shore of Valcour Island, I described the island's history, and told them the story of Smuggler's Cove, and how it came by its name because bootleggers carrying boatloads of illegal whiskey down the lake during prohibition, hid in the cove to escape detection by revenuer patrol boats. I informed my tour passengers that many of the town's wealthier families today owed their good fortune to an ancestor who wasn't afraid to run a load of booze down to New York City. Today Smuggler's Cove is a popular haven for boaters wishing to escape rough water on the lake or perhaps picnic on its pleasant beach or take a swim.

We were constantly looking for ways to make the cruise more enjoyable and decided serving food would be a real enticement. Serving food proved a plus and as there is a natural demand for drink to accompany food, I applied for and obtained a liquor license. We had food and a full stocked bar but the only food we served consisted of three sizes of steaks. This made the handling of tickets complicated because we had to sell three different tickets. The price of each ticket depended on which steak the passenger selected when purchasing their ticket. It was confusing. We eventually cured that problem by offering passengers their choice of a 9-ounce Delmonico, or 9-ounce Shell-steak, which we could provide at the same price.

It was brought to my attention that we needed approval from the Clinton County Health Department to provide food on the Juniper, so I went to them and asked what needed to be done for certification. They thumbed through their regulations and couldn't find any that pertained to the sale of food on board a vessel. They were in a quandary as to what to do, so I wrote out a plan of operation applicable to the service of food on vessels plying the waters of Lake Champlain, and gave it to them. They looked it over, couldn't find anything wrong with it, and issued me a restaurant license.

Juniper Dinner

At that time there were only ten tour boat operations in all of New York State, and most of them had catered stuff that they brought on board and served from steam tables. I was the first that wanted to cook meat on a charcoal grill mounted on the stern of the boat. Of course cooking on board presents a safety question and I gave the issue serious thought. By mounting the grill on the stern, if something went wrong (with the grill), we could tip it off the back end of the boat and put the fire out. The Coast Guard wouldn't let us use propane grills and they were not all that popular at the time anyway."

Of course, providing passengers with a memorable meal required hiring a chef, who could cook large quantities of food on a grill, positioned on an often rolling deck and have that food come out to perfection. Frank knew the perfect individual for the job. He was the son and namesake of the one time owner of the Valcour Marina, where Frank had opened his original dive shop. Billy Reid adored Frank Pabst and he quickly accepted Frank's offer of employment. An article penned by Shawn Ryan and published in the *Plattsburgh Press-Republican* on September 16, 1999, under the caption *"Juniper Chef Loves His Job"* provides a vivid description of Chef Billy Reid: "Finding a professionally trained, worldly- seasoned chef in the Plattsburgh area is certainly not impossible. Finding that chef behind a grill on the bow of a converted cargo ship on Lake Champlain, however, might be some cause for surprise. That surprise quickly dissipates after an evening's outing around Valcour Island on the dinner cruise of the Juniper. There, anchored off picturesque Valcour Island with the sun setting over the Adirondack mountains, head chef Billy Reid puts his nearly 30 years of cooking experience and commitment to service on display. Reid, who graduated from Peru High School in 1968, knew from an early age that cooking was in his future. 'As I look back, just about everything was geared toward that,' remembers Reid, whose earliest experience in the food-service industry came at his father's Tastee-Freeze at Peru's Harborside. After high school, Reid went to college to pursue a chemistry degree. While at college, he took a work- study job as cook. 'It was there that I really became aware that I wanted to be a chef.' Reid left college and returned to the North Country to take a job at the Sportsman's Club in Wilmington. There he experienced being a professional chef under the tutelage of Carl Steinhoff, a family friend and well-known area chef who would become Reid's mentor. 'The main thing Carl Steinhoff taught me was to love serving people, that and he taught me a lot about cooking. None of his recipes were written down. They were all just monkey-see monkey-do' said Reid. After getting his feet wet at the Sportsman's the Draft Board came to Reid, and he served a year and a half in the military as a radio repairman. When he returned from the service, he came back to the Sportsman's, but knew eventually he wanted to go back to school. Utilizing the GI Bill, Reid entered the Culinary Institute of America in 1974, and graduated in 1976. After returning home from the CIA, Reid worked for a time at Valcour Lodge, Apple Barrel in Peru and D&H Restaurant in Plattsburgh, as well at the Pacific Café on Fisherman's Wharf in California, to name just a few of his stops. 'I just kind of worked around, worked here and there, I did the things I enjoyed doing. I started going to Florida in the winter time and eventually ended up in Naples in the early '80s.' In Naples, Reid found a different world for a professional chef, away from the cozy confines of home. 'Naples was full of these private clubs, these walled-in communities. No longer was I the head chef. These Florida clubs were full of European chefs whom everyone was in awe of,' said Reid, who quickly gained the respect of the Europeans. Reid still returned to his beloved Lake Champlain during summers, living aboard his boat. He became guest chef aboard the *Juniper* for his friend Frank Pabst for special occasions, and, in the summer of 1998, Pabst invited Reid to be his chef full-time, a job Reid gladly accepted. 'I like being around here because we get to point out a lot of the history of the lake. I get to get up and talk to people,' said Reid of his tenure on the *Juniper*, adding, 'the cooking part is enjoyable, but the serving part is still what I like most, seeing people enjoy their dining experience. It's what Steinhoff used to call ' a culmination of details.' Those details intertwine nightly with the rippling waves and majestic sunsets of Lake Champlain to culminate in a dining experience topped by very few'."

Those who know Frank particularly enjoy the way he spices an innate propensity for oratorical flair with quaint quips applicable to the matter under discussion. During our many meetings his out-of-the blue utterances forced me to smile and I began to look forward to the next emanation of wit. I was awed by the sudden displays of proverbial genius from a man who dropped out of school at an early age. When I asked Frank how he managed to keep the *Juniper* cruise going after losing so much money during its first year of operation, his immediate response evidenced eternal optimism.

Frank chuckled and responded, "After achieving a life long dream, I refused to let it turn into a nightmare. Man does not live on bread alone, and although being broke, I could scrape up enough change to buy bread – or get it free from my good friend George Bouyea, owner of Bouyea Bakery – and we scraped up enough money to buy milk – and of course, beer. I also had the support of a loving wife, the support of many loyal, good friends, who contributed both labor and money to keep the *Juniper* afloat. I had faith in the *Juniper* too. She was old, but she was rugged and I knew in my heart that the business would start turning a profit. One of the things that kept me going was faith in me by the President of the Keeseville Bank. He was a fine gentleman and President of the Chamber of Commerce at the time. The bank loaned me $40,000 and I put the *Juniper* down as collateral. Some time after I received this loan, The Keeseville Bank was bought out by a foreign bank – I think it was the bank of Hong Kong – and I was contacted by a lawyer working for this new bank, who informed me that the bank was forbidden by a law, known as the Jones Act, from holding a vessel under U.S. flag as chattel. This meant that for all intent and purposes, the bank was hanging in the wind, and relying on my honesty to pay off the loan. Well, we managed to make payments on the loan, although I have to admit that during the Carter years, when interest rates soared to 24%, we had difficulty just making the interest payment. However, eventually after a few years the loan was satisfied and the bank was very appreciative that we didn't stiff them. That was one of two loans that we wound up getting on the *Juniper*. The second loan was obtained after a fire nearly put us out of business."

At reflection of the fire, Frank's beaming face suddenly displayed a look of sadness and his blue eyes revealed a hint of moisture, but only for a brief moment, because his warm personality would not allow even this sad event to pull him down. He digressed from the telling of the *Juniper* just long enough to relate the circumstances of two disastrous fires that nearly put Heritage Adventures out of business.

"In 1978, we had our first fire. It destroyed the house trailer that we used as our office and set fire to the end of the railroad warehouse. The fire occurred at night and the cause was never discovered - although the point of the fire's origin was established and it was surmised that during a cold snap the seizing up of an over-heated electric clock, started it. The warehouse contained paper that the *Press-Republican* used to print their newspaper. After the fire, we bought the paper from the newspaper, got a floor sander, sanded the burned edges of the paper and then sold it to a recycling plant up in Canada. We came out making a $1600 profit on the paper. I used that money to get our smoke-damaged chairs and life jackets cleaned. We were hit with a second fire in 1984 more disastrous than the first, and this time the cause was suspected as arson. That fire cost me $250,000 and we lost just about everything on shore, but we managed to save the *Juniper*. Fortunately, by this time I had investors solidly behind me. We recovered, rebuilt and I got permission to place two mobile homes on the property from which to operate. Sadly, that fire not only destroyed business records, but photographs and memorabilia from our early years of operation. All of our life jackets and most of our deck chairs were damaged by soot. To clean them, I set up a horse trough, filled it with a mixture of water and strong alkali solution, and heated the trough with a hot water heater from a barn. We scrubbed the life jackets in the trough, then tied them all together into a bundle and attached the bundle to the rear of the *Juniper*. Then we took the *Juniper* out onto the lake and towed the bundle of life jackets around to rinse them off. Unfortunately, the alkali solution that we used to clean the deck chairs was so strong it destroyed the threads on the chairs. They were ratty looking but I didn't have money to purchase new ones, so we got them through another year. Recuperation from the fire was slow, but it was good. We came back stronger and better. We perfected our menu and our on-board kitchen and introduced chicken, swordfish and salmon as dinner choices. On special occasions, we also served passengers 'surf and turf' and lobster tails."

The author would venture a guess that during the approximate 25years of the *Juniper's* service on Lake Champlain as a tour boat, hundreds and perhaps thousands of tourists, as well as nearly every resident in the Champlain Valley had walked her deck. I would imagine, that like me, they marveled at a scenic mountain vista that can only be fully appreciated from out on the lake, where the beautiful Green Mountains of Vermont on the east, and the rugged Adirondacks to the west are portrayed together on one living canvas. Those passengers like me, also took delight in Captain Frank's history lessons, and thrilled at his stories of lake legend and lore, or, if not history buffs, they enjoyed a temporary respite from the summer heat by standing on the *Juniper's* bow to savor a cooling lake breeze, oftentimes made cooler by spray from huge waves breaking over her prow. Or perhaps they enjoyed eating excellent food, prepared by on-board chef 'Billy Reid,' and being able to imbibe in adult beverages in an uninhibited atmosphere. Captain Frank particularly enjoyed hosting private parties on the *Juniper*, because the number of passengers attending each event was known in advance, and those cruises were usually quite profitable. The *Juniper* was ideal for an intimate private party, as she became a floating café, or restaurant, where patrons could relax and party in an open-air atmosphere having a delightful ambiance.

Over the years The *Juniper* hosted numerous weddings, engagement parties, bachelor parties, birthday parties, retirement parties, promotional celebrations, business trips, political campaigns, school field trips, etc. I can imagine that the *Big Bottle's* designer, shipbuilder, former Captain(s) and crew would be amazed at the once-floating Pepsi dispenser's transformation. In boating lore the '*Juniper*' could be likened to the fairy tale 'Cinderella.' The story of an over-worked, ill-cared for young river freighter that was transformed into a respected Queen of Lake Champlain. I can also imagine that Captain Frank and the *Juniper* were destined to find each other, because both Captain and ship were products of New York City and during their early life both had toiled in New York City. Both eventually made their way to beautiful Lake Champlain, where they found each other and romance blossomed.

The *Juniper* faithfully served her master as a tour boat and performed double duty as the mainstay of Captain Frank's lake salvage business as well. Over the years she was used in some memorable ship recoveries and construction projects including installation of a water system for Swanton, Vermont, and the dredging of the Chazy River.

Frank is proud of these accomplishments and took joy in relating the events. "The second year I had the *Juniper* in service, I got a call from Charlie Anderson, a friend who owned New England Marine Contracting. Charlie employed an engineer by the name of John Wisner, who used to dive with me. Charlie told me that he had obtained the contract to install a water system for Swanton, Vermont. The contract called for placement of water intake pipes in Lake Champlain. The water conduit had already been installed down to the lakefront, and now the water intake pipe had to be placed in the lake. That year there was quite a bit of ice on the lake. In December, the wind was especially fierce – rising to 80-knot gusts – and it pushed the LCM and barge used for the work up on shore, destroying the

LCM. The loss of the LCM stalled out the project, which was already running way behind its anticipated completion date. In the spring, Charlie called me and asked for my assistance. On April 14, 1978, we went over with the *Juniper* to start laying pipe. After getting set up, I discovered that the employees for New England Marine would arrive for work about 7:30 in the morning, work until 9, then stop for coffee break. On return from coffee break, they worked until about 11:30 a.m., then left the job site, traveled into town for lunch and returned to the job at about 1:30 in the afternoon. Consequently, there wasn't a hell-of-a lot of work getting done for several hours during the day. I cured that problem by serving coffee and lunch on board the *Juniper*, eliminating a lot of wasted travel time. We did the work and brought the job in on time."

After completion of the Swanton water project, Charlie leased his LCM to a company based in Syracuse, New York.

Frank recalls, "A company out of Syracuse, New York obtained the contract to dredge the entrance to the Chazy River. They came up here with a mud cat, which is an auger dredge, and it was hitting a lot of obstruction that it couldn't move. They were looking for help and came to me. They rented a 90-foot barge from the Lake Champlain Ferry Company. Then we erected a floating boom around the barge and placed a Caterpillar 235, having a 3yard bucket on the barge. Then we loaded a 10-wheel dump truck on board the LCM and towed barge and LCM out to the dredge site. Five scoops with the Cat bucket loaded the truck. When it was loaded, we brought it back to shore. The loaded truck drove off the LCM, another truck drove on and we hauled it out to the dredge site. This job was behind schedule when we started and we brought it in on time."

Despite her age, the *Juniper* was a rugged ship and her diesel engines were powerful. Captain Frank was frequently called upon to use the *Juniper* to salvage sunken vessels.

"The *Carew Two* hit Hog Back Rock Reef and sank," Frank recalls. We went over with the *Juniper* to see if we could salvage her. I attached winches on the 'knees' of the *Juniper's* bow (square eye beams affixed to the front of the vessel) and we winched the *Carew Two* up off the bottom of the lake. Then using the *Juniper's* power, we pulled the ship into Shelbourne Bay where it was raised by a crane. Also, after hurricane Floyd, the *Juniper* participated in salvaging boats that had gone down over in Shelbourne Bay. Sailboat skippers love the sort of stiff breeze that fills their boats sails, but an ill-wind never blows any good and every time the wind churned up huge waves, we were called upon to either rescue sinking vessels, or salvage those that went down."

A native of Plattsburgh once told me, "Frank Pabst knows more about Lake Champlain than any other living human being." I had to agree, because in our many hours of conversation, Captain Frank displayed a superb knowledge of every island, cove, shoal, reef and hidden rock in the magnificent lake that stretches 120 miles in length and is 11 miles across at its widest width. I asked the Captain how he came by his knowledge of the lake's many hidden dangers.

He smiled and blue eyes revealed a hint of mischief, as he responded, "I learned about most of the hidden dangers from other sailors smarter than me."

"What do you mean, smarter than you?" I naively asked.

"Well, they must have been smarter that me, because they discovered the hidden dangers before I did, then called me to come salvage their boat. After pulling boats off stones and low spots, you remember where they are." Having said this, he laughed out loud and added, "Actually, I faithfully follow my lake charts and on-board radar."

It would be virtually impossible to operate a tour boat for nearly a quarter of a century on Lake Champlain without experiencing a gamut of unexpected incidents. The Juniper's logbooks serve as testament and reminder of too many unexpected events encountered on the lake. While perusing the logbooks, I could imagine the thrill experienced – not by the crew, but - by the many passengers witnessing a boat rescue, person rescue or 'Champ' sighting. The event was certain to be forever etched in their minds, whereas such events were almost commonplace for Captain Frank and his crew. The brevity of Captain Frank's logbook entry regarding each incident – like the tempting aroma emanating from the kitchen of an excellent cook – made me hunger to learn more about the particular events. These are some of the teasing tidbits from the Juniper's Logs:

May 24, 1978 – 40' twin diesel ran aground on breakwater.
Rammed off w/Juniper.
May 25, 1978 – small run-about ib/ob ran aground on
breakwater. Went out w/lobster boat and

rescued them.

August 5, 1979 – Towed in sailboat *'Obsession.'*

September 24, 1979 – On return to P-burgh from Westport rescued 3 people from overturned canoe. Took them to Basin Harbor.

June 29, 1980 – Red flares @ Valcour – boat on reef.

July 25, 1980 – Salvaged 30' sailboat on Hogback Reef (Sunset Island).

July 11, 1981 – VIP boat for Mayor's Cup.

July 11, 1984 – female passenger dove off west of Valcour Light – executed recovery search.

June 26, 1985 – Assault on board by college kids.

August 16, 1995 – A female passenger @ arrival dock from night cruise reports having seen a passenger jump off the port side some 1 ½ hour previous to report. Unfounded.

August 15, 1999 – recovered 1814 Bateau. Took to base.

August 19, 1999 – recovered 1814 Bateau. Took to base.

The brevity of the written entries made me wonder if they had been written by the same Captain Pabst who converses using a brilliant display of clichés and adages and who holds listeners spellbound with adventures and stories of Lake Champlain.

Frank explained, "Shucks, I didn't feel a need to elaborate in my log, and you know sometimes a written record – in the hands of the wrong person – can come back to haunt you. My log entries were adequate reminders of the events."

Some of the incidents were reported in the *Plattsburgh Press-Republican,* and a search of microfiche found the reporter's portrayal of the events.

For example, on August 21, 1999, Editor Susan Seguin reported the recovery of the bateaus in the Plattsburgh Press-Republican. Her article appeared under the title *"Bateau Finding Lucky,"* and states as follows: "Capt. Frank Pabst thinks dredging in Plattsburgh Bay may have aided the recent discovery of two bateaus. 'There's a wealth of history being uncovered there,' he said. 'I think the wall they've installed (for the dredging project) may have changed the current flow. It's washing away sand that for years hasn't been washed.' Pabst should know. As skipper of the *Juniper* excursion ship he has plied local waters for 40years. His docks are on Plattsburgh Bay. Pabst tells of a 1774 relic explored some years ago by city firefighter Gary Brandstetter in 12feet of water. Two days later, when Pabst and Brandstetter returned to the wreck, the water was 6feet deep. That means 6feet of sand had washed in in two days. Some think the lower lake level may also have helped. Due to the lack of summer rain, Lake Champlain's water level is 94.4 feet, about a foot lower than normal, according to the National Weather Service in Burlington, Vt. But Plattsburgh State geologist David Franzi thinks lower water has little to do with the findings: 'I can't think of anything different in the lake that would account for finding the two boats.' He attributes the discoveries to serendipity. The bateaus, believed to be part of the fleets that took part in the Battle of Plattsburgh on Sept. 11, 1814, recently came to light. One find, consisted of planks that could be placed together to form the bottom of a bateau - a flat-bottomed boat commonly used in those days to transport men and supplies. The second discovery, made this week, revealed a complete bateau bottom. 'It was in superb condition, intact, the entire bottom is together,' Pabst said. 'It was a fantastic find. It reinforces the rich history we have here.' He participated in efforts Thursday to move the bateau bottom to deeper waters, where State Police divers weighted it to hold it on the bottom of the lake, to be preserved until it can be properly restored. The artifact was discovered within 4feet of the shoreline. It was covered with 12-14 inches of sand, lying under just a few inches of water. Volunteer workers, with permission from the state, carefully unearthed it. 'We took an initial outline, and we uncovered the material layer by layer. We had the opportunity to take readings and make drawings of everything we found as it lay in the sand,' said Keith Herkalo, who spearheaded the effort... 'There were no circular saw marks on the planks. They were sawed with a two-man crew, one above and one below in a pit, or one on ground level and the other on a raised platform. They started at one end of the log and worked to the other end, so there are saw marks all across the face of the boards. Each is in excess of 20 inches in width. This bateau was a little different from the first one. It has a square stern, whereas the other was pointed. We have a piece of the caulking that was used between the boards. It is either horsehair or cotton. And we recovered many iron nails. One is almost 7 inches in length. It was found about 14 inches from the bow of the boat. It could have been used to hold the bow stem.' Herkalo was effusive in praising the judgement of Dannemora correction officer Steven Lacey, who discovered the ruins. Lacey notified experts before disturbing the find. 'The best example we could have is what he did. He didn't dig it up. He didn't move it. The way something lies may tell a story. Wood is incredibly spongy, but because it was not pulled on or moved, everything remained intact. We found a button (a small brass U.S. Navy uniform button lodged in a crack). It could have disappeared into the sand. And that little button, that could so easily have been lost, is a powerful piece of history. Being part of a naval uniform, it ties the bateau almost certainly to the Battle of Plattsburgh."

When asked to expound on the occurrences so briefly cited in the *Juniper's* log, Frank ran a hand through his mane of thick silver hair, chuckled as he reflected on each event - then related, "Well, probably the incident that readers will be most interested in happened on our August 26, 1985 night cruise. I ended up accidentally shooting my 1st mate that night."

Having said this, Frank paused and waited for my reaction, while displaying a sheepish grin.

I just stared at him with a stone-faced stare, because it seemed so many peculiar things happened in this interesting man's life, that nothing surprised me.

He continued, "A bunch of teenagers from Keeseville took the cruise that night and they were bad kids. They gave us a real hard time on the entire trip. Harry Horton was my 1st mate and also my good buddy. I worked for him after I left Channel 5. At the time I was deputy director of Civil Defense for the City of Plattsburgh. I would wear a suit in the daytime and report to an office. Come six o'clock, I donned coveralls and got behind the wheel of a four-axle hauler. I hauled sludge from the sewer plant up to the landfill in Altoona, and Harry was my boss. I did that for about 2-years after which, I quit the civil defense job to run the *Juniper*. Harry signed on board as my 1st mate. Anyway, these kids were causing trouble on the boat and we took them back to the dock. When we arrived there, heated words were exchanged and one of the kids knocked me down and stomped on my finger. Just two weeks previous, I had an accident down in Westport, during which I lost the tip of that finger when it became caught in a V belt. The finger was healing fine until the kid stepped on it. A wave of excruciating pain surged through my hand and up my arm. I had a .32 pistol on me and I pulled it out, intending to shoot in the air to frighten the kids and take command of the situation. When I pulled it out, the kid kicked my hand and the gun went off. The bullet struck Harry in the arm. Harry getting shot caused the kids to panic and they all scrambled off of the boat. Fortunately, Harry's wound wasn't serious and he recovered without holding any grudge against me. The Plattsburgh police investigated and the end result was that I had to surrender my weapon. I told them that as I was Captain of the boat and a member of the Clinton County Sheriff's Department, I was entitled to have it. I really didn't need to use that argument, because I've also got a valid pistol permit. The incident was written up in the newspaper, but I don't have any copies of that one.

On May 24, 1987, we were in the process of closing the *Juniper* down from our evening cruise and heard a noise coming from the direction of the breakwater. We looked in that direction and saw a red and green light in the dark. A 38-foot steel diesel boat had struck the breakwater. The boat was impaled on the rocks and the Captain couldn't move the vessel backward or forward. We went out with a small boat and brought the Captain in to shore. We told him that come daylight, we would use the *Juniper* to get his boat off the rocks. Fortunately, the lake was calm and was expected to remain calm through the night. We knew that it would be easier to free the boat during daylight and there was no rush to get the boat off the breakwater because it wouldn't be pounded against the rocks by waves. I called the Coast Guard to report the boating mishap and asked the Canadian boat owner/Captain if he had a chart of Lake Champlain. He replied that he did and produced a 'road' map of the eastern United States, which depicted Lake Champlain like a coffee stain. I tried not to laugh, and wondered how he managed to get from Montreal to Plattsburgh without mishap. The following day we went out with the *Juniper,* bumped the boat off the breakwater, then brought it in to my harbor and chained it to a tree. All of a sudden law enforcement agencies started descending on us like crows to road kill. Customs, Border Patrol, Quebec Provincial Police, New York State Police all made an appearance and told me they were going to seize the boat that we had just removed from the breakwater. It seemed they were investigating the reported theft of the boat. I argued that they could not seize the boat until my salvage fee was paid. I would point out that a boat's documents are the Bible for the boat. In this case, the boat's ownership was in question. Mr. A owned the boat and sold it to Mr. B. Mr. B wrote A a check, then promptly sold the boat to Mr. C. The check B gave to A bounced and when he confronted B for the money, B told him, 'It's not my problem since I no longer have the boat. Mr. A then went to C to get his money and C left him sitting in the office while he supposedly was going to get the money. Instead, C went down to the harbor in Montreal, and started south toward Lake Champlain. He got as far as Plattsburgh before running the boat on to the stone breakwater. As it turns out, the boat remained in my care and custody for over a year. When the question of ownership was finally resolved the boat didn't look too bad, but it had weathered badly and it wasn't worth anywhere near what it was when A sold it to B. Mr. A from Canada got his boat back and we ended up getting somewhere between, $6000 - $7000 for storage.

"In 1977, John Ianelli was Mayor of Plattsburgh. John had a great love for the city, was well liked by most of its citizens, and worked very hard at improving the quality of life here. More importantly to me, John, harbored no aspirations for higher political office, recognized that my tour boat was good for Plattsburgh, supported our operation from the city waterfront, and didn't hassle me with oppressive regulatory enforcement. If there was a problem or concern with our operation, John called, or made a personal visit, we discussed the problem, and worked out a solution. John was no phony-baloney politician, but a real fine gentleman who could be trusted. Such would not always be the case. A successor to Mayor Ianelli gave me a very hard time and tried to put me out of business but I'll address that later.

As I previously mentioned, we went severely into the red during our first year of operation, but we were determined to make a go of it. During the spring of 1977, as we were getting the *Juniper* spruced up to commence tour operation, Mayor Ianelli informed me that the City had decided to attract tourists and boost lake activity by hosting an annual 'Mayors Cup Festival and Regatta.' The centerpiece of the planned festivities would be a sailing regatta, with the winner presented the Mayor's Trophy. I was ecstatic when Mayor Ianelli asked that the *Juniper* be designated VIP boat for the race and invited me to participate on the committee planning the event. I agreed – without hesitation – and the *Juniper* proudly served as VIP boat for the Mayor's Cup for a number of years. Whether it was the VIP boat or not depended on who was Mayor at the time. Since it's advent in 1977, the annual event has expanded and grown into a weeklong celebration in downtown Plattsburgh. The group of dignitaries responsible for establishing the program for the Mayor's Cup seemed a little bit stodgy. What I mean by that is that they were a group of Philadelphia lawyer types who owned fancy, expensive sailboats. After meeting with them and listening to the strict rules and regulations they were establishing for the event, I felt that a little bit of levity should be added to the event, so I suggested that a 'Crazy Craft' race should be included and I would offer a prize to the winner of the event. The criteria for participating in the Crazy Craft contest consisted of launching anything that floated and wasn't mechanically propelled. The participants would launch from the lighthouse, go to the breakwater and finish at the mouth of the Saranac River. The craft design was left to the imagination of the entrants and there was a variety of truly crazy designed craft. One entry consisted of a guy in a bathtub using a canoe oar; another was nothing more than a cardboard box; another named the *Yellow Submarine* consisted of a plank attached to two 55gallon drums. The Tijuana Jail launched a raft with a mechanical donkey on it, whose tail lifted and spewed balloons out its rear end. The race was won by one of my crew aboard a banquet table supported by inner tubes and using two tablecloths from my restaurant as sails. The prizes were: 3 cases of beer for 1st place, 2 cases of beer for 2nd place and 1 case of beer for 3rd place. Our 'Crazy Craft' race attracted more attention than the serious sailboat race, as a crowd gathered on both sides of the river to cheer the participants. The attention given this hilarious race, ruffled the feathers of some members of the sailing club, who wanted the festival to focus on the sailboat race, but by the end of the day, their egos were massaged and they held no grudges."

It is no secret that throughout the near quarter of a century the small section of leased lakeside property that went by the name of Heritage Inc., having its office located within a railroad repair yard, more resembled a junkyard than a tour boat operation. The visual condition of the premises caused some Plattsburgh residents and politicians to grumble and complain that the property was an eyesore. What Frank's detractors failed to realize was that Captain Frank was not exclusively in the business of operating a lake tour boat. A rigging and salvage business and diving business were conducted from the same premises, and much equipment and craft was needed to conduct these businesses. Minus a plentiful supply of operating capital, Frank purchased old boats and equipment that he could afford, made the repairs needed to keep them in use and, when they were not in use, they appeared as unsightly clutter to narrow-minded individuals. Frank did his best to keep his premises neat and attractive; however, at times the accumulation of old boats and salvage equipment cluttered the property.

Frank explained, "The people complaining about me and my operation failed to realize that I needed a lot of equipment to run my business, and I had little room to store it and virtually no money to pay for storage. In addition to the *Juniper*, I had cranes and tugboats and we were doing marine contracting. Throughout the years my relationship with the City was tenuous. Some administrations treated me with respect and left me alone, and others harassed me and tried to put me out of business. I tried to cooperate with every administration though, because experience had taught me that trying to butt heads with politicians and bureaucrats is a dead end street. I promoted the undeniable fact that the *Juniper* boat tour brought tourists to downtown Plattsburgh and made money for the City. When I started up the boat tour, what I had was a diamond in the rough. I just didn't have the money needed to polish it, and my attempts to polish it by advertising were frustrated by many different levels of government. My business was a plus for Plattsburgh, but the City never gave me any help. They would schedule events on the *Juniper* from time to time – Mayors Ianelli and Renell used the *Juniper* as VIP boat for Mayor's Cup races - but for the most part, we had an adversarial relationship, and no show of appreciation for what I had done. Every time I tried to put a sign up to advertise our boat tour, the City and Town of Plattsburgh forced me to take them down. The Town of Plattsburgh's justification for denying me advertising was that the *Juniper* wasn't in the Town so they really didn't care about it. Yet, I hired kids who lived in the Town of Plattsburgh. I went to one of the town meetings and told the board as that was their attitude, I would just fire all the kids working for me who live in the town and tell them that their town officials are responsible for their losing their jobs. I went through the trouble of obtaining agreements with property owners along the Northway to place signs advertising our boat tour on their property. After going through the expense of having the signs created and erected where they would catch the eye of motorists, New York State came along, tore down all my signs and informed me that I could not place advertising in view of the Northway, because state law did not provide for the advertising of tourist attractions. This seemed ridiculous and arbitrary to me, because the law did permit advertising for hotels, motels, restaurants, etc. That law has since been changed.

Trying to work with the City of Plattsburgh was even worse. After we got the tour boat up and running, I spoke with Bob O'Neill, the owner of a meat packing business located on Bridge Street and contracted to place a billboard on top of his building. The city made me tear it down. So, I purchased a 25-foot helium-filled balloon and I tied that on top of the O'Neill building. The balloon could be seen for miles and it said 'BOAT TOURS.' The City went ballistic over that and ordered me to take it down. I argued that I was a dirigible pilot and parked my dirigible on top of the O'Neill Building. The City didn't find any humor in my response and still ordered me to take it down. So, I took it down and moved it to the Tijuana Jail Restaurant. Occasionally, we tied the balloon to my VW and drove around town. It was a sight to behold. At times I wondered if a sudden gust of wind would cause the balloon to lift the VW off the ground. The City fought me tooth and nail over every attempt at advertising my business, but for some reason, the helium balloon garnered the most ire from them. We tried many schemes, including painting advertising on a truck and parking it in the Day's Inn parking lot, located at the major Northway exit into Plattsburgh, and the Town forced its removal. We placed a sign at the intersection where the Northway empties onto Route 3, and the state or town tore that down. Despite all the regulatory and bureaucratic stumbling blocks, the Dock and Coal Marina was an ideal location and a comfortable marina, so the City and *Heritage Boat Tours*, co-existed in a usually friendly environment. However, after Clyde Rabideau became Mayor, he wanted the land that my business occupied. He started putting pressure on us in the hope of forcing us out. He had the building inspector down to our property so often that I told him I was going to declare him as a dependent on my income taxes. Mayor Rabideau had me cited for code violations and forced me into court. However, my attorney managed to thwart the Mayor at every corner.

It seemed we were always in some sort of 'catch 22.' The City should have been overjoyed to have the *Juniper Boat Tour* because in essence it was a historical Renaissance that promoted the history of the area and brought in money. I think that on the one hand, 'they' were happy that the *Juniper* was bringing people to Plattsburgh; however, on the other hand, 'they' did nothing to support this Renaissance, and worse, fought my efforts to make it more successful. It didn't make sense to me. I was operating a legitimate business, promoting the history of the area, not hurting anyone or interfering with any other business and government kept erecting barriers. Having to get the permits, play 'mother-may-I' and jump through hoops for various people who, didn't have a clue what I was doing for the betterment of Plattsburgh, was costly and frustrating. Of course, the folks involved in erecting the 'hoops' had good intentions but much of the permit process was totally prohibitive to progress. It was additionally frustrating because the whole historic aspect of Plattsburgh - the historical awareness that Plattsburgh is now enjoying - started with my efforts. Many people helped along the way, but I feel that I was the catalyst that got it started."

Frank is always eager to point out his love of history and how important Lake Champlain is to American History.

"This area is rich in history." Frank proclaims. "During the exploration of North America, when the primary mode of travel was by ship, the lake was a strategic water highway where many confrontations occurred between first the French and British and later between the British and American Revolutionists. The majesty and beauty of this lake attract tourists to a lake cruise; however, treating them to a history lesson doubles the pleasure of the cruise and makes it more memorable. To promote lake history, we donated a lot of cruises to worthy causes. For instance, when I learned that students from Beekmantown School had their travel money ripped off by an unscrupulous travel agent, we hosted a fundraiser on the *Juniper* and the kids raised $1500. I offered to let them sell tickets for a boat tour and they could keep 100% of the money they collected. I was happy to help them out, but also knew the food and soda sales to 100 passengers on the tour would at least permit us to break even and not lose money. The kids got their cruise, made money and we broke even. We were delighted to provide this service.

We also supported various political fundraisers aboard the *Juniper* and, during our many years of operation, the *Juniper* hosted important history-making events, attended by many dignitaries."

One of these events included the get-together of New York's Governor Mario Cuomo, Vermont Governor Madeleine Kunin and Quebec Premier Robert Bourassa to sign a memorandum of cooperation to clean up Lake Champlain. Various media witnessed the moment, and the *Plattsburgh Press-Republican* would announce, *"Kunin, Cuomo Sign Agreement to Clean up Lake Champlain."* The accompanying article written by Meg Dennison of the *Associated Press*, reported, *"Aboard the Juniper* – Drifting along the border of Vermont and New York, the governors of the two states and the premier of Quebec Tuesday signed a memorandum of cooperation to protect Lake Champlain. The agreement, two years in the making, "signals a new commitment to environmental protection," said Vermont Gov. Madeleine Kunin, who initialed the pact. "It provides a wonderful opportunity to show we act beyond state and provincial boundaries," Kunin said. New York Governor Mario Cuomo, who joined Kunin and Quebec Premier Robert Bourassa under Tuesday's sunny skies, heaped praise on Kunin. "It's a good thing that Gov. Madeleine Kunin has the leadership and initiative to reach out," he said. Premier Robert Bourassa and Quebec Minister of Environment Clifford Lincoln also joined in signing the agreement, though Quebec will participate in the agreement's terms only as needed, officials said…Tuesday's agreement, the first formal statement of cooperation on lake issues, recognizes increasing pressures on the 120-mile long lake, 60 percent of which is controlled by Vermont and the remainder by New York and Quebec. Industrial and residential discharges as well as agricultural runoff have threatened the lake's water quality, while rivers feeding into it have been dammed," Kunin said… The four-year agreement calls on environmental officials of the states to trade information on water quality, air quality, lake water levels, recreation, fish and wildlife development, solid waste management, pesticide applications and hazardous waste management…"

Politicians on Juniper part 1

Politicians on Juniper part 2

Frank chuckled as he reflected on an aspect of this tour that he now feels free to share with readers. "I was honored and felt proud to host this come together of 'big wigs' aboard my boat. We gave them a grand tour and I think they enjoyed themselves. During the cruise, I managed to capture Governor Cuomo's ear for a short private chat. He thanked me for hosting the event and complimented me for caring about the lake and making its beauty available to tourists. I thanked him in return and encouraged him to consider passage of legislation that would allow casino type gambling on board cruise vessels operating in the State of New York, similar to what was already permitted in other states. Of course, I pointed out that a hefty state tax on the operation would make a lot of money for the state. The Governor told me to submit my proposal in writing to his secretary. He would look it over and give it consideration. I submitted my proposal as requested and received the standard response thanking me for my letter. My proposal was probably quickly filed in the 'round' file, because that was the last I heard of it, although I did receive a letter from Governor Cuomo thanking us for putting on a great buffet.

Experienced sailors on Lake Champlain are aware that calm waters can turn suddenly ugly on any given day and do not challenge its power.

Captain Frank summed up the power of the lake in classic Pabst style. "Most of the time the lake is a serene beautiful seductress but 'she' can become ugly on only a few minutes notice, producing huge waves that can turn a lulling cruise into a 'rock and roll' adventure. Usually, being 63 ½ feet long and having a 30-foot beam, the *Juniper* could handle pretty rough water; however, there were times when she was buffeted and tossed about like a cork by an exceptionally angry lake. One trip was exceptionally memorable. It was fall, and we were heading over to Vermont for haul out. I had all types of stores on the boat, and just off Providence Island, we hit some really rough seas. One huge wave curled over the *Juniper's* bow, hit the front doors, blew them open, swept down the length of the deck, smashing legs out from under tables, knocked over a 50-lb. box of potatoes and these potatoes were scattered everywhere. Fortunately, the doors weren't broken and we managed to survive that storm without significant damage. Another time, we were out on a reserved cruise for Pepsi Cola employees. They ended up having quite a memorable cruise. A storm hit the boat, blew in the front door and knocked the refrigerator over. It landed atop a lady seated in a chair. She caught the 'fridge' and luckily it wasn't that heavy and luckily, she did not get hurt. It was a bad storm and we rode it out with a lot of luck that no one got hurt. All considered, the *Juniper* experienced more damage from passengers than from storms. We had two passengers who kicked the doors, putting their foot through it and each time it cost us about $500-$600 to repair the damage. Once back at the marina, we reported the damage to the police but on both occasions the District Attorney refused to prosecute the person responsible."

Despite her age, the *Juniper* kept going like the pink rabbit in a television commercial advertising a certain battery, and under the loving care of Captain Pabst, she could have continued service as a tour boat for many years; however, the City of Plattsburgh wanted to emulate the City of Burlington Vermont in development of its waterfront, and to do so, they felt it necessary to take control of Captain Frank's property and introduce a grand, elegant tour boat similar to the 500-passenger *Ethan Allen*, which was based in Burlington.

The push to retire Captain Pabst and the *Juniper* was hardly a smooth transition and, in fact, could be equated in seaman's terms to sailing in shifting, uncertain winds on a very bumpy sea. This analogy was made readily apparent in a series of articles appearing in the *Press-Republican* between February 2001 and April 2002. City leaders had drooled with envy over Burlington Vermont's waterfront area and envisioned creating a similar setting in Plattsburgh. Before that could be done, they had to acquire ownership or control of the Canadian Pacific rail yard and that parcel of prime lake front property controlled by Captain Frank. That would not be an easy task.

Frank Pabst was a controversial enigma – having a host of supporters and handful of detractors, most of whom, did not really know him personally and either disliked the messy appearance of the property he controlled, or were jealous that he controlled it. One city administration had used intimidation and harassment to try and force Frank into retirement. The administration's relentless attack under the guise of enforcing various zoning, state and local laws took a monetary and psychological toll on both Frank and Ann Pabst; however, 'they' underestimated the intelligence, pride, stubbornness and resiliency of the *Juniper Captain* and his wife. The Pabst's quietly and efficiently successfully resisted every tact used by the city to dispossess them and continued running their business while dodging pails of mud thrown by pawns of the city bureaucracy.

"Mayor Rabideau tried to accomplish the City's goal by applying pressure and forcing me out of business." Frank explained. "I fought back and thwarted his every move. His successor Mayor Dan Stewart was a little more diplomatic. He and the City Council decided the best way to put the *Juniper* out of business and obtain control of my piece of waterfront was through buying me out."

The Stewart-led city administration wisely took a friendly, more diplomatic approach to win Frank over and used kind words and monetary inducement to convince him that retirement was in his best interest. During the period of negotiation with Frank to purchase his lease, city officials gave several interviews to the *Press-Republican*. Some officials praised Frank and thanked him for his service to Plattsburgh, others issued conciliatory statements, while grumbling about the process.

In the February 6, 2001 issue, *Staff Writer Jo LoTemplio reported under the title "Waterfront Cleanup a City Priority:* If City of Plattsburgh Mayor Daniel Stewart's visions for sprucing up the downtown waterfront come to fruition, residents won't recognize the place this summer. "In the summer of 2001, the waterfront will be a totally different looking area," the Mayor said. "I think once people see what we are doing down there, they will really enjoy it and be less resistant to changes." The mayor's plans, which he will unveil today in the State of the City address, call for major changes to the waterfront. Chief among them will be the replacement of longtime boat captain Frank Pabst and his legendary *Juniper*. The city is working on a deal to buy Pabst out of his lease with Canadian-Pacific Rail and eventually lease the dock space to another cruise-boat company out of Burlington, Vermont. As part of the deal, the city will clean up Pabst's lot, which has become a salvage depot for old boats, vehicles, appliances and all kinds of equipment. "We will miss Frank Pabst," the mayor said. "You may not like his yard, but you have to respect a businessman like that who has been in business for so long and survived. He has become a legend. With Pabst gone," Stewart said, "the path would be cleared to not only host a larger cruise boat, but to create a public boat launch and recreation area. For me, the major focus of this administration is to open up as much waterfront property as possible," Stewart said. Pabst, 69, is all in favor of the move. After running the *Juniper* for 25 years, he is ready to start a new chapter in his colorful life.

"As much as it's time for me to move on and do different things in life, it's time for this property to move on as well," Pabst said.

The city is looking at paying Pabst between $125,000 and $150,000 to buy him out of his lease with CP rail…The mayor says the investment is well worth it…Before any cleanup of Pabst's yard begins, he will have the mother of all yard sales.

"Everything down here works, Pabst said. It may be old, but it still works." With Pabst and the Juniper cleared out, the city will lease the dock space to a new cruise line in the summer of 2002…"

Frank attests, "At 69 I was wearying of fighting bureaucracy and had started considering retirement. Having been self employed most all of my life and never having made much money, I was staring at old age without any sort of a pension, and a buy out by the city would give my wife and me something for old age. I also thought that the City's plan to turn the waterfront into an attractive park and convention center was a good idea, so I informed them that if they came up with a reasonable offer, I would retire the *Juniper* and they could buy me out. Eventually, we came to terms, and I put the *Juniper* up for sale.

On May 26, 2001 a *Plattsburgh Press-Republican article titled, "City To Vote On Pabst-Juniper Buyout"* reported: "City councilors will decide next week whether to buy out longtime boat-tour captain Frank Pabst. The move could be the first step in totally revitalizing a prime piece of lakefront property in the city…It appears councilors are leaning toward supporting the $125,000 deal with Pabst…Pabst, the colorful sea captain, has run Juniper Boat Tours near the mouth of the Saranac River for 25 years. He has been leasing the property from Canadian-Pacific Railroad and has right to continue the lease. The city is looking to forge ahead with an ambitious plan to redevelop the entire area near the mouth of the river. Stewart has laid out plans that would include moving the Canadian-Pacific rail yard and re-locating the Water Pollution Control Plant and the Municipal Lighting Department yard. "But," the mayor says, "it all begins with buying the rights to lease the waterfront property from Pabst, who would like to retire. The city has put together a deal that would give Pabst $25,000 for the rights to lease the property and $50,000 a year for two years to keep him on as a consultant to waterfront issues. "Frank has a wealth of information about the lake bottom in that area, and he would be very valuable." The mayor continued, "With the Juniper gone, the city will bring in the Ethan Allen II tour boat from Burlington, VT. The city has an agreement with the Ethan Allen II for a 10-year lease, and the revenue from that deal would go toward paying back the $125,000 that is going to Pabst..." "Anonymously, some councilors griped about having to 'pay for Frank Pabst's retirement,' but it appears there will be enough votes to approve the deal..."

Several members of the city council continued to grumble and complain about having to buy Frank out, but in the end they joined Mayor Stewart and in May 2001 unanimously agreed to the buyout. On June 1, 2001 the *Plattsburgh Press-Republican* reported that decision under the headline *"Handing Over The Helm..."* "After some debate about the terms of the contract, the councilors authorized the Lake City Local Development Corp., a development arm of the city, to ink a $125,000 deal with Pabst, who has operated boat tours on Lake Champlain for 25 years. Under the contract, Pabst would be paid in return for the right to lease the waterfront property he's rented from Canadian-Pacific Rail, cleaning up the 1.2-acre site off Dock Street and remaining as a waterfront consultant for two years."

"I'm a happy man, and I really do think the City of Plattsburgh will be the overall beneficiary of this," Pabst said after Thursday's vote.

While pleased with the outcome, he was, however, a bit agitated about the hemming and hawing of some councilors over the deal.

"I've done a lot for this city over the years, and now I'm being treated as a cancer that needs to be cut out. I would have hoped that it would have been more respectful and more of a handing-over of the helm type of thing."

At the start of the council meeting, Councilors Harold "Rebel" Hicks and Jack Stewart spoke out against the agreement that they argued was hastily written and left questions about liability and cleanup unanswered.

"I want nothing left there that will cost the city one penny," Hicks said of the equipment, vehicles and buildings that must be removed by Pabst over the summer.

Councilor Stewart also argued against any deal that would allow Pabst to keep his aging boat, the *Juniper*, at the dock until the end of September. "That's a problem," he said.

Two residents hoped to change the councilors minds. The Rev. John Sorenson of Trinity Episcopal Church urged them to consider the importance of the waterfront and what a new boat tour would do in attracting tourists. He told the council that the second most asked question he receives from travelers, besides how to get on the Interstate, is the location of the city's access to Lake Champlain. And, Sorenson said, "Approving the contract would demonstrate a show of respect for Pabst, who has worked as Captain of the *Juniper* for more than two decades. He's done it with grit, determination and not too much money. I believe he deserves our respect for his vision."

Resident Michael Kulik also extolled Pabst's long-term commitment. "The deal is in the best interest of the city," he said.

"Moments later, when it came to vote on the matter, all five councilors were behind it…"

Following the vote, several councilors voiced their reasons for approving the buyout and in general agreed that putting control and development of the waterfront in the hands of the city was the priority.

"A staunch proponent of the deal, Mayor Daniel Stewart applauded the councilors' unanimous decision. The vote here tonight adds to the Spirit of Plattsburgh," the Mayor said, referring to the name of the new boat that will move into the Juniper's spot next summer. Mayor Stewart also lauded Pabst for, among other things, raising from Lake Champlain the anchor from the *Confiance*, a British warship defeated during the Battle of Plattsburgh. The anchor is now displayed in City Hall, outside the council chambers. "I think that anchor is worth $125,000 alone," he said.

Having reached agreement on the transfer of his lease to the City of Plattsburgh, Frank began the task of removing all of his property from lakeside and on October 11, 2001 the *Plattsburgh Press-Republican* reported under the catchy headline, "*Stewart: A Blue-Ribbon Pabst.* Work on a new boat dock to house the Spirit of Plattsburgh will begin next week. The dock is part of a $500,000-plus project that will transform a portion of the city's waterfront near Plattsburgh Harbor Marina at the end of Dock Street. "So far, things have been going to plan, and it's looking good," Mayor Daniel Stewart said Wednesday… The dock construction will involve a new sea wall and space large enough for the *Sprit of Ethan Allen* to dock comfortably…Pabst, who was paid $75,000 initially by the city, said cleanup of his yard is nearly complete. He will get another $45,000 from the city once the job is done…While he agreed to the deal, Pabst is not thrilled with the way it transpired. Before agreeing to the deal, the Common Council vigorously debated whether it was wise to pay Pabst.

"They (councilors) have been treating me like a hemorrhoid for years and couldn't wait to get rid of me," Pabst said. "Nobody ever said thank you for running boat tours and teaching the history of the lake for 25 years."

The Mayor said Wednesday that he was grateful for Pabst's business. "I am sorry to see him leave because he was one of the most colorful personalities that ever graced the shores of Lake Champlain," Stewart said. "He did provide a great service, but now it's time for a new chapter."

The pain filled expression of sadness on Captain Frank's face as he described selling the *Juniper,* could be equated to the look displayed by one who has just lost great love, and he whispered, "It was one of the saddest days of my life; however, I found some cheer when she was purchased by my good friend, Tom Cross. (Log book states 'to M& Nancy Cross)"

Before being dry-docked, the *Juniper,* under control of her venerable captain, would perform a magnificent task that would proudly create a whole new chapter of Lake Champlain history. A task that bestowed honor on boat and captain and ensured they would not be forgotten. The Juniper cruised out into Cumberland Bay and raised from the bottom of the lake the most famous ship anchor in American history. The British warship *Confiance's* anchor, severed by American Commodore McDonough's gunners on October 12, 1814, was hoisted to the surface and delivered to historians in Plattsburgh. This was perhaps the finest hour in Frank Pabst's life and one that deserves a full chapter in his life story.

On October 12, 2001 – ironically, on the 187th anniversary of the defeat of the British in the Battle of Plattsburgh - Captain Frank made his final entry in the *Juniper* Log. That brief entry is a sad footnote to the *Juniper's* distinguished career. Terse and simple it states, "Final move to Wilcox Dock."

Many City residents were elated that the *Juniper* and its Captain had – in a sense – been forced into retirement. They saw Frank as a contentious, stubborn man standing in the way of lakefront beautification. However, Frank's supporters far outweighed his dissenters, and as it became known that the era of the *Juniper* was about to end, this is some of the commentary that appeared in several editions of the *Plattsburgh Press-Republican:*

Feature Editor Greg Claus wrote the following critique of the city's actions under the headline, *"Councilors Should be Pleased with Pabst Deal.* Most people are familiar with derivations of the sayings and/or clichés: They can't see the forest for the trees and It's all a matter of perspective. (I'm not sure the second is a cliché or even a saying, but, for the sake of argument, let's just say that it could be one or the other or both) The City of Plattsburgh Common Council will come to face with both bromides Thursday evening when it decides whether to pay Frank Pabst $125,000 for his lease with Canadian Pacific Railroad and to procure his services as a consultant for two years. Pabst, the longtime captain of the *Juniper,* will get $75,000 upon signing. He'll pocket another $45,000 60 days later, provided he has cleaned up the area around his dock. The final $5,000 check will get cut at the end of the summer after the cove is cleaned. The agreement will further put Pabst in a binding, non-competitive arrangement with Lake Champlain Scenic Cruises – the *Spirit of Ethan Allen,* which stands poised to sign a 10-year deal with the city. Any rumblings the councilors have about the deal or the cost should go away. They should agree to the deal, and they should do so happily...For starters, 125 grand for what the city will get is not a lot of money. In fact, it's a steal. Taxpayers will not have to fork over dime one. The money will come from the local Community Development Office in the form of a loan that Lake Champlain Scenic Cruises will pay over the course of its contract with the city. Now here's where the forest-for-the-trees part comes in. Some members of the Common Council may not like paying Pabst to clean up his boat yard and take possession of the lease. Too bad. Pabst has given the city and the Champlain Valley more than he has gotten in return over the last several decades. From salvage work to rescues to Plattsburgh's floating lake historian to his legendary Booze Cruises, the colorful captain leaves a legacy of service that will be missed. But, for those who are unmoved or simply don't like the man, remember this: He controls the lease. If the city wants to control the waterfront, it has to possess it first. This deal is just one part – albeit a vitally important part – of the city's plan to turn the waterfront into the jewel of the city. Without it, the efforts that came before – The Heritage Trail, the development of the Naked Turtle, the bike path and the Riverwalk – could well be rendered meaningless. Certainly, CP will have little motivation to move the rail yard if the deal falls through. And, without a change of address for the yard, any further waterfront-development plans are dead in the water. And, while it appears Mayor Dan Stewart already has the votes he needs, if the council gets behind the proposal enthusiastically, it will send the right message to the state, the federal government and, most important of all, to the residents it serves."

Appearing in the *Lake Champlain Weekly* was this barbed snippet: *"Snipers In Plattsburgh.* City Council, are taking cheap shots at Captain Frank Pabst from behind a wall of anonymity over the city's proposed plan to buy out his waterfront lease and hire him as a consultant, saying that they don't want to "pay for Frank Pabst's retirement." Sounds like people who not only have the verbal venom of a Portugese man-of-war, but the vertebrae as well."

By the spring of 2002, salty-tongued city waterfront consultant Frank Pabst began running into trouble with Mayor Stewart, who formerly had only words of praise for him. The source of agitation had to do with damage to the expensive new dock the city had built for the *Spirit of Plattsburgh.* The incident was reported by Staff Writer Joe LoTemplio, in the April 30, edition of the *Plattsburgh Press-Republican* under the caption: *Concrete Solution Needed –Tourboat Dock Cracked; Cause, Remedy Pursued.* "The City of Plattsburgh's high-profile waterfront project has hit a serious snag in the form of a damaged dock. Several cracks have formed in the newly pouted concrete seawall that is used to tie up the city's new cruise ship, the *Spirit of Plattsburgh.* Also, several of the wood planks nailed to the dock posts were smashed to pieces last Thursday, when high winds relentlessly slapped the 120-ton boat against the dock. Mayor Daniel Stewart said it is unclear, though, whether the cracks in the concrete wall were caused by the boat banging against it or from the earthquake that occurred Saturday, April 20. "This a problem, but it's not going to jeopardize or even delay the project," the mayor said. "It's a glitch that we will deal with and take care of." The mayor said a breakwater off the shore of the dock would probably have prevented the boat from banging up against the dock. The U.S. Army Corps of Engineers is scheduled to install a new breakwater this year. Surveys for the project were completed last summer. Stewart said he called Congressman John McHugh last Friday to see if that project could be expedited. "The bottom line is that we need a breakwater and we need it now," he said. The city's $315,000 waterfront project is being touted as the first step in transforming the Plattsburgh Harbor Marina area near the mouth of the Saranac River. The project is being paid for largely by state funds and will include a kitchen facility for the cruise ship, a parking area and the new dock... The mayor said that he believes the weather was the major culprit, "We had some nasty weather on the lake last week, and a lot of people on the lake had some damage, and we are in that same situation," he said. One waterfront expert, however, says the whole problem could have easily been avoided.

Frank Pabst, the longtime captain of *Juniper Boat Tours*, which operated from the dock site for 25 years, said he warned city officials that a concrete dock would not work. Pabst, who was bought out by the city last summer for $125,000 to pave the way for the new project said, "The dock needs to have some give to it to absorb blows. The dock I built cost $1,500. It might not have been pretty, but it lasted me 25 years. You don't have to be a rocket-scientist to figure out how to build a dock."

The mayor said Pabst's Monday-morning quarterbacking does not help solve the problem. "Now is not the time for Frank Pabst to be spewing public comments about this situation," Stewart said.

Frank expounds, "I guess I was a 'consultant' to the city in name only. In reality the Mayor and several city council members were not interested in anything I had to say about development of the waterfront. I had suggested how the dock should be constructed but they either didn't hear me, or ignored me. They wanted a dock that looked elegant, but didn't put much thought into the power of an angry lake and how it can create waves that can smash even a huge ship against its docking."

This is a smattering of the letters that would appear in the local newspaper: *"Capt. Pabst the Kind-hearted.* To the Editor: I would like to thank Greg Claus for writing 'Councilors Should be Pleased with Pabst Deal' in the May 27 issue of the *Press-Republican*. In it he mentioned several of the positive things Pabst and the M/V *Juniper* have done for the Champlain Valley, including rescue, historical events and the famous "Booze Cruise." Having sailed with Capt. Pabst for 18 years, providing entertainment for the Dinner Cruise, I'd like to add a few things that many folks would otherwise never know. When the French Club at Beekmantown High lost their hard-earned money for their trip to France, it was Pabst who donated 100 percent from a cruise that helped to recover their loss and ensure their trip. His children never attended Beekmantown schools. Every year Pabst provided special rates for the ARC and its clients to enjoy the beauty of Lake Champlain and its tremendous history in the founding of our country. Senior-citizen groups from all over the North Country were always given a sizable discount to compliment their fixed incomes. Raising the anchor from the British ship "*Confiance*" that was lost at the Battle of Plattsburgh Bay cost Pabst in excess of $7,000. He's still waiting for a formal "thank you" from the City Hall. The beautiful bronze cannon that's on display at Clinton Community College was also raised at Pabst's expense along with its sister cannon on display at the south end of the lake. There's not clearly enough room within the boundaries of "Letters to the Editor" to do Pabst's services to the North Country any justice, but having witnessed many of them first-hand, I had to pass a few of them on for all to see." (Robert Wesley, Dannemora)

Editors note: Robert Wesley, like Frank Pabst, was born in New York City, led a diversified life, moved to the North Country in search of a better environment and fell in love with Lake Champlain. Unlike Captain Frank, Wesley is a talented musician and an accomplished chef. In 1980, while attending Plattsburgh State University, where he majored in computer science, Wesley met Captain Frank Pabst, they became instant friends and the Captain asked Bob if he would like to provide the musical entertainment on the *Juniper* for the summer. What started as a one-season gig would last for 18 years and Wesley attests that it was the best job he ever had. In a tribute published in the *Plattsburgh Press-Republican* on December 29, 2004, Wesley told reporter Kevin Couture, "Going to work wasn't always easy, but it always turned out to be enjoyable. I'd be at home a lot of times and I'd say, I really don't want to go to work again, but after I got to the boat and I got my equipment set up, it was the best job you'd ever want."

Under the title, *"Kind Words About Pabst." To the Editor:* Sometimes we only realize the value of something when it's gone. The kind words about Frank Pabst were important for family and friends. They now tell how much was lost to the greater community. As you state, now may be the time to act on one idea; now may be the time to remember one man." (Walter Forst, Brooklyn)

Under the title, *"Pabst Has Made a Difference, To the Editor:* I would like to wish a fond farewell to my good friend, Capt. Frank Pabst. Mr. Pabst is legendary – a character who will be sorely missed. Frank Pabst has worked very hard for many long years in promoting tourism in Plattsburgh. He has a wealth of knowledge and has contributed so much to historical record keeping, including donating artifacts, his time, expenses, labor, etc. I believe the buy-out price to be a fire sale. I told him he should have asked for double – Lake Champlain waterfront, after all, is very expensive. Capt. Frank Pabst – salute. You are proof that one man can and does make a difference." (Kathy Rock, Keeseville)

Under the title: *"Recognition Past Due, To the Editor:* Just a note of thanks for your editorial on Friday, April 18 – It was good to see Frank Pabst getting some recognition for the work he has done in keeping our history alive. I would hope that when and/or a naval museum is ever established here that the contributions Frank Pabst has made are acknowledged." (B. Wingler, Cadyville)

Under the title: *"Pabst Will Be Remembered, To the Editor:* As with any significant event, people are sure to reflect on what impact this has on both themselves and those around them. Such is the case with the retirement of Frank Pabst, and I'd like to add my sincere thanks and best wishes to those of many others. Frank's contributions to Plattsburgh have gone unnoticed by many of us yet have influenced us all. Visiting friends and relatives have always commented on what wonderful times they have had during their *Juniper* cruises and have made it a point to enjoy the experience again when they returned. It gave visitors to the area – as well of many of us residents – the opportunity to realize the scenic beauty of our Lake Champlain basin. I'll miss the call of the *Juniper's* horn across Cumberland Bay. Frank's salvaging of historical artifacts from the depths of Lake Champlain, have brought life to the legacy of the Battle of Plattsburgh. Because of his efforts, Frank has given something that visitors – as well as those living in the area – can enjoy and take pride in forever. As a champion of small business, Frank has always been known for his straight talk, hard work, honesty and integrity. I've always admired his courage to stand by his convictions. In an age where these personal traits are dwindling, it's never easy to see people of this character move on. Change may be inevitable, and, as I welcome the proposed improvements to the waterfront, I also urge each of you to remember this man and what he's done for our community. Smooth sailing, Skipper." (Byron Ordway, Cumberland Head)

The *Editor of the Plattsburgh Press-Republican* paid this tribute to Captain Frank in the paper's June 5, 2001 edition: *"Pabst Legacy In Bright Future.* Frank Pabst sat alone in his office in the shadow of the spiffy *Ethan Allen II* tour boat last week while community leaders boarded that liner for lunch and a tour of Plattsburgh Bay and beyond. The boat so dazzled the assemblage, that Pabst's *Juniper* seemed more a rowboat than a tour boat. But it was Pabst and the *Juniper* that, for 25 years, were our only link to Lake Champlain and the vistas it represented. As a diver, he showed us the treasures the lake cradled for safekeeping. Michael Shea brought his *Ethan Allen II* from Burlington to Plattsburgh for a luncheon ride around several historic miles in Lake Champlain. Shea, calling Plattsburgh "an emerging city," told the gathered he'd re-christen that boat *The Spirit of Plattsburgh* and begin regular cruises in 2002. That seemed like spectacular news to almost everyone on board. The boat is a multi-level, enclosed brush with luxury, in comparison with Pabst's smaller, open one-time ferryboat – a Cadillac next to a VW. Passengers envision *The Spirit of Plattsburgh* as an answer to the area's prayers – a legitimate tourist destination by which buses would drop their riders, who typically spend $5,000 throughout the community per busload. The city looks forward to the day *The Spirit of Plattsburgh* permanently takes to the lake from the city's dock. It will truly be an exciting new entrée on the menu of local activities from which to choose. It will enhance the area's growing dual attractions: history and fun. Meanwhile, though, let's not forget Pabst and the *Juniper*, who, it begins to appear, will soon be out of sight and out of mind. Pabst has rankled many in the community with his unorthodox ways and maverick spirit. In his view he fought with the city over placement of signs promoting his business – and promoting the city at the same time. The collection of salvage and assorted junk on his lakefront lot is not a pretty sight and must be cleaned before the city will consummate its deal with him. But give him credit for being a pioneer for all the recent initiatives that aim to imbue the area with new vitality and prosperity. Pabst has not historically been well treated by his city – in some ways, with good reason, and in many, not. But don't lose sight of the fact that he was struggling to exploit the good idea of lake tourism before the rest of us knew what a good idea it was. He deserves our thanks and a felicitous send-off."

In 2002, the following advertisement in the *Plattsburgh Press-Republican* caught the eye of this author and in a sneaky way it seemed to take an un-needed swipe at Captain Pabst and the *Juniper*. The ad: "The *Spirit of Plattsburgh* offers a magnificent ship for full menu cruises for brunch, lunch, dinner and later. It refines and enlarges the venue created by the now-retired and long memorable Frank Pabst 25 years ago with his *smaller Juniper tour boat."*

On 5/03/2002, *"The Spirit of Plattsburgh,"* an elegant 500 passenger, 3 deck cruise ship, after much advertising, ballyhoo and fanfare, embarked on its maiden voyage from the Plattsburgh dock. Captain Frank had not been invited to participate in the festivity.

Frank recalls, "When the *Spirit of Plattsburgh* arrived in Plattsburgh, I was over in my yard, within sight of the festivities, cutting up steel."

Mayor Dan Stewart saw me, came over and asked, "Frank, how come you are not on board the boat?"

This last minute invitation struck me as sort of callous and I responded – probably in a tone of voice that reflected how I felt, "Because you didn't invite me."

"Well," Dan responded, "You are certainly invited and I would like to have you come along."

I was dressed in work clothes, dirty and sweaty from working on the pile of steel and because I looked like a bum, I did not want to join all the well-dressed dignitaries on the vessel. So I responded, "Dan, I am all dirty and you want to bring me on the boat so people can point their fingers at me and laugh. Thanks, but no thanks."

Author's comment: During the following year, my wife and I took four dinner cruises on the *Spirit of Plattsburgh*, and coincidentally, we had taken four cruises on the *Juniper*. We mutually agreed that although the large cruise ship was elegant, there was something missing. The *Spirit of Plattsburgh* frankly lacked SPIRIT, and we did not find the same degree of ambience that we had enjoyed on the *Juniper*. We asked ourselves why, and came to the conclusion that what was lacking was Captain Frank's personality, his lake history lessons, his many yarns, and the closeness and camaraderie of passengers and crew on the smaller boat. On the *Spirit of Plattsburgh*, we were just part of a large crowd on a big boat operated by a young Captain and crew who could not communicate the rich history of the lake or its surrounding area. Speaking frankly, if, we had not been accompanied by friends our cruises on the *Spirit of Plattsburgh* would have been boring. It did not surprise us that upon conclusion of the 2003 season, after two years of service, the owner of the *Spirit of Plattsburgh* announced that the *Spirit of Plattsburgh* was a losing proposition and would not return to Plattsburgh in 2004.

As of this writing, although Plattsburgh is moving forward with its plan to develop the waterfront, the city is without a tour boat.

Crab Island

The Captain of the Juniper was familiar with every island on Lake Champlain, but one 40-acre, physically unappealing expanse of limestone rock, covered with dense forestation and poison ivy, fascinated him more than the lake's many more attractive islands. The attraction was the island's location, just one mile south of Plattsburgh, and the fact that the island is steeped in history. History-loving business entrepreneur Captain Pabst envisioned developing the island into a park that would attract tourists, honor its history, and of course increase business for the *Juniper Boat Tour.*

Crab Island, once named Saint Michel by the French during the era they controlled Lake Champlain, played an important role as a military hospital during the War of 1812, specifically, during the Battle of Plattsburgh, which occurred on September 11, 1814. Wounded sailors and marines from both American and British ships were taken to Crab Island and treated at a field military hospital established there. Many would die that day, and they were hastily buried in shallow graves on the island. Historical documentation reflects that 149 or 150 American and British seamen are interred on the island.

Frank is quick to point out that practically all the islands in Lake Champlain are steeped in history. For example, "Father Jacque's island located near Westport, was named after French priest Father Jacque who was a missionary and his mission was to convert the Indians dwelling along Lake Champlain to Christianity. Apparently, he was not too successful. One day the Indians invited Father Jacque to dinner. Unfortunately, he was surprised to learn that he was to be the entrée. The island located near where the martyred priest met his tragic demise was named after him. However, Frank attests, beyond any doubt, Crab

Island is the most historic island in the lake because of that fateful time on a fall day in 1814. I believe historic Crab Island could serve as an important tourist draw to Plattsburgh and the Champlain Valley, if properly developed and taken care of. Instead, he snorts with disgust, after erecting a magnificent granite monument and flagpole on the island to honor the dead and memorialize the isle's important role in the shaping of America, the government failed to enact any provisions for the care and upkeep of the island, thereby letting the island fall into disrepair. The monument was vandalized, and the flagpole rusted and collapsed. Years of neglect caused dense growth proliferated by poison ivy to make the island inhospitable and virtually impassable to humans. Many folks in our community – myself included – were disgusted by the government's abandonment of that hallowed ground. We believed that the island could be much improved and serve a much greater historical role, under private ownership, but of course that didn't seem possible because government owned property is seldom returned to public or private ownership. I frequently visited the island, cleared poison ivy from the vicinity of the monument and was angered by the government's abandonment of what could and should be an attractive historical park, inviting to both picnickers and tourists. I often sat at the base of the monument and tried to envision the hectic scene on the island that fateful day in 1814. It seemed fascinating that the island was selected as a neutral territory for the creation of a hospital to treat the wounded from both American and British forces, and that it just sort of spontaneously happened from immediate need and not as part of a planned battle strategy. I can imagine that if a medical doctor was on the island that he was overwhelmed by the enormous task of trying to treat wounded numbering in the hundreds. I can envision the wounded and dying lying on the rocky shore; hear their moans, hear a murmured chorus of prayer begging for healing or salvation of their soul. I can envision many pairs of blue, brown, hazel, gray, green eyes displaying both physical and emotional pain, mixed with fear, as life ebbed from their bodies and the realization set in that they would never see their loved ones again, and that the destination of their soul was in the hands of the Almighty. I see them as brave and courageous men, many still in their teens, much too young to die, and wondering if their sacrifice had been made in vain. I can hear the echo of the roar of cannon-fire and envision clouds of smoke roiling across Cumberland

Bay and smell the pungent odor of burnt gunpowder. I often wonder what the shaping of America's northern boundary would have been if not for a lucky cannon shot that severed the mighty *Confiance's* anchor, turning the tide of victory to the outmatched and outgunned American fleet. I can imagine that if the British had been victorious in the Battle of Plattsburgh that Crab Island would today belong to Canada. Surely, the Good Lord was on the side of the Americans that day because the British naval and land force descending on Plattsburgh and Cumberland Bay outnumbered the American forces by more than 2 to 1. The Battle of Plattsburgh was more important to the shaping of America than most present day citizens realize and Crab Island played a significant role in that historical event. While sitting in reflection at the base of the monument, I envisioned how I would develop the island into a tourist attraction if I owned it. At the same time I knew that this was just wishful thinking because the government would never give up ownership. Therefore, I was really surprised when in 1967 a notice appeared in the paper that the government had declared Crab Island surplus and was offering it for sale to the highest bidder. I yearned to purchase the island and had great plans for developing it, but all I could scrape together for a bid was $8000 and that wasn't enough."

Crab Island Monument

The following brief advertisement appeared in the *Plattsburgh Press-Republican* on June 8, 1967: "Crab Island will be offered for sale by United States government on June 16, 1967."

On 12/5/67, the *Plattsburgh Press-Republican* reported: "Edward Troise who resides in Pennsylvania has purchased Crab Island for the sum of $40,200."

"I did not know Mr. Troise, had never heard of him, and had no idea why this gentleman from Pennsylvania wanted to own Crab Island," Frank attests. "I hoped to get to know Mr. Troise and learn what he planned to do with the island, but that did not happen." Displaying a momentary whimsical look of sadness he added, "After buying Crab Mr. Troise didn't seem to make any effort to warm up to the Plattsburgh community, and didn't openly discuss with the media what he planned to do to improve the island's condition. The years passed and it appeared that this gentleman from Pennsylvania who owned the island, had no intentions of making it more appealing to the public. It continued to become more overgrown with brush and ivy and increasingly grew more inhospitable. While cruising past the island on a daily basis, I thought, *'what a waste of historically valuable real estate.'* From time to time, when 'we' felt overly ambitious, 'we'd' go out with wet suits on and cut the poison ivy that was around the monument, so that at least the monument remained visible. Other than having poison ivy and brush cleared by a group of concerned citizens who cared about the island, nothing was done with it for about 18 years. Then in 1985, Mr. Troise sold Crab Island to a wealthy business entrepreneur from New Jersey by the name of Walter Jakubowski."

A very brief article in the Plattsburgh Press-Republican announced the sale: "Edward Troise has sold Crab Island to Walter Jakubowski, a wealthy New Jersey businessman for the sum of $190,000."

This sale, unlike the previous sale, stirred into action a group of residents led by Plattsburgh City Historian Jim Bailey, opposed to private ownership and development of the island. They began stirring up a hornet's nest of opposition to the sale, petitioned the state to take possession of the island, and publicly and privately voiced their opposition to any development of the island for commercial purposes. Their opposition ignited a spark of controversy that naturally captured the attention of the local news media. This article appearing in the *Press-Republican* on September 16, 1986, expressed opposition to the sale and served notice on Roger Jakubowski that he could expect his ownership of the island would be short lived. Staff writer Jack Downs wrote: "It appears that the New York State Office of Parks, Recreation and Historic Preservation will not intervene in the sale of Crab Island to New Jersey businessman Roger Jakubowski. We have checked with the realtor involved and at the current time have been foreclosed from continuing in a competitive bidding process, said Deputy Parks Commissioner Ivan Vamos on Monday. Vamos also said that the state could only make its offer based on the appraisals it had received, and didn't feel it could get involved in a bidding war with an escalated price. Vamos said that the state did offer considerably more than the appraisal of $150,000. Although he wouldn't discuss specific numbers, it is believed that the state's offer was nearly $170,000 and Jakubowski's successful bid was about $192,000. Located just off of Cliff Haven in Lake Champlain, Crab Island is a 40-acre uninhabited tract that is the gravesite of about 50 American soldiers who died fighting in the 1814 Battle of Plattsburgh. It also contains a monument to these war dead. A number of years ago, while under the administration of Plattsburgh Air Force Base, it was sold by the federal government as surplus property, the graves apparently forgotten. The island and its history were "rediscovered" early this year by City Historian Jim Bailey when the island came up for private sale. He began a public push to get the island purchased and protected by the state. The state had the money to do it from funds left over from the 1972 Environmental Quality Bond Act. Also, the state department of environmental conservation had just reached agreement this summer to purchase the final private parcel on Valcour Island, Crab Island's sister island to the south, and a plan had been worked out for a ranger to oversee the upkeep of Valcour and Crab Islands and the state public boat launch in Peru. However, Jakubowski's bid has apparently brought an end to these plans.

"It appears that the sale price is higher than what we are able to make an offer on at this stage," Vamos said. He added "the state will get in touch with Jakubowski and with local people who support the island's preservation and see what can be worked out, but the state cannot interfere with the Jakubowski contract now except by eminent domain. The state does have two appraisals in hand that could be used for this purpose that are "in disparity" with Mr. Jakubowski's offer." In other words, by using eminent domain, the state could proceed with a forced sale using these appraisals for a price of around $150,000 rather than the $192,000 offered by Jakubowski. However, if the state took the island using these appraisals, Jakubowski could appeal and cite his own reasons why the island is worth more. If the court agreed with him, the state could wind up paying "very dearly" for the island. We provided the best offer we could give," he said. "We are considering what to do next."

Frank hoped to get acquainted with the island's new owner and managed to do so through the auspices of a good friend. "Peter Guibard, the owner of a foundry in Plattsburgh, was a good friend of mine," he relates, "and Peter had made the acquaintance of Roger Jakubowski. Peter was impressed by the way I did things, and he impressed me by the many things he had accomplished. We liked and trusted each other and had discussed how Crab Island should be developed. Peter had taken Jakubowski out to Crab Island, explained the island's history, and Jakubowski saw that with cleanup and proper care the island would be beautiful, and he fell in love with the place. Peter introduced me to Jakubowski, and I was immediately impressed by his exuberance and perception of how important Crab Island was to the history of the lake. Standing at about five-eight or five-nine, Roger was not physically imposing, and although of middle age, like me, he had totally white hair and folks who didn't know us might easily assume we were brothers. I was also impressed by his entrepreneurial spirit and willingness to invest in the future of Plattsburgh. We seemed to immediately take a liking to each other and in fact, he hired me to investigate ways to open the island to the public. We began to forge an excellent relationship. Roger had the money needed to develop the island, and I agreed to invest my time and effort into the project. The longer I knew Roger, the more I liked him. (As a matter of fact, I worked for him just about a year ago (2002). He owns 'North Country Spring Water' located down in Port Kent, and he needed some minor work done.) Getting back to Crab Island – I wasn't an investor in 'Crab Island Development Company,' but I was a participant in the project, reporting to Roger, who was the main man. We decided to clear the underbrush and ivy; then, create a picnic area and walking trail around the island. I would operate a shuttle boat, taking tourists to and from the island. Our ultimate goal was to open up a museum on the airbase, operate a shuttle boat to the island, which would include telling passengers the story of the 'Battle of Plattsburgh' and pointing out the significant history of the island. Our long-term goal was to commercialize the island and if the law changed to permit it, put a gambling casino out there. Of course, Roger's plans for developing the island drew the attention of the anti-private ownership hornets and the ire of some residents, who were opposed to any commercial use of the island. These dissenters began raising a stink and claimed that the 'sanctity' of the island would be violated. This argument seemed nonsensical to me, because after erecting a monument and flagpole on the island, the government abandoned the island's sanctity, letting the flagpole collapse, letting vandals damage the monument, and poison ivy to take control of the ground. Jakubowski's plan called for clearing the ivy and dense growth from the grounds to make the island inviting and hospitable to humans. His plan was environmentally friendly, didn't leave any toxic waste, made the island attractive and habitable for humans, and paid homage to the island's history. The truth be known, these dissenters were leery of an outsider taking control of the island and turning it into a profitable investment."

Unsuccessful in their efforts to stop the sale of Crab Island to Roger Jakubowski, the anti-private ownership crowd took another course of action and started putting pressure on local government to rezone the island to prevent Jakubowski from developing it. They captured the ear of members of the Town of Plattsburgh governing council who decided that Crab Island needed to have zoning restrictions and of course, the zoning issue was reported by the local media. Under the banner "Island Called Safe from Over-development" *Press-Republican Staff Writer Downs wrote,* "Although the Plattsburgh Town Board may need two months to decide if Crab Island will be zoned, Supervisor LeFevre said Monday that the island is safe from over-development. Millionaire Roger Jakubowski, who outbid the state of New York for Crab Island last week, will be unable to take title to the land and begin construction before the town decides on a land-use plan," LeFevre said.

Regardless of zoning, Jakubowski will need a planning-board site-plan review, a town building permit and other state permits before any development could begin," said Town Zoning Enforcement Officer William Flynn. "These permit procedures that Jakubowski faces will make it nearly impossible for him to build before the town fully considers zoning," Flynn added. When that consideration is made, Crab Island would probably fit into the "land conservation" land-use classification, a very restrictive zoning category that allows little more than golf courses, riding stables and parks.

At Monday night's regular board meeting, councilmen forwarded to the town planning board three letters advocating zoning for the island and asked planning board members to consider the case at a Sept. 23 meeting. Accepting this late item on their agenda Monday, town board members made it clear that the possible zoning of Crab Island is a priority for Plattsburgh...LeFevre acknowledged the possibility that restrictively zoning Crab Island, effectively cutting the value of the property, could bring legal action from Jakubowski. "However," LeFevre and Flynn said Monday, "that the town's attorneys have advised them to proceed toward zoning. Until then, Crab Island remains the only land in the town not covered by a land-use plan."

Captain Frank recalls the "shenanigans" pulled by various levels of government to prevent development of Crab Island with disgust and a sense of outrage. "It is a well known adage that a squeaky wheel usually gets greased," he related, "and the group of dissidents squeaked and squawked very loud capturing the attention of the Plattsburgh Town Board. The Town of Plattsburgh promptly acted to enact zoning regulations that severely restricted development of Crab Island. Of course Roger Jakubowski was outraged, as well he should be. He had fallen in love with that 40-acre pile of poison ivy covered rock out in the lake and had good intentions to make it attractive to tourists and local residents, and as a businessman, make some money on his investment. He had the misfortune of having the reputation of being successful and hailing from New Jersey. If a 'north country good old boy' had purchased the island with a plan to develop it, in all likelihood, he would have stood a stronger chance of prevailing against the dissidents. Interestingly, when the GSA sold the island to Mr. Troise, they neglected to include a covenant in the title to preserve the monument. Roger's development plan included preservation of the monument, and construction of a fence around the cemetery where the 1814 combatants were buried. If Roger could not develop the island, that preservation would not occur."

In 1986, less than one year after Jakubowski purchased Crab Island, the island was zoned 'historic' and zoning regulations severely limited what the island could be used for. An article in the November 7, 1986 edition of the *Plattsburgh Press-Republican* reported: "Town Zones Crab Island Restrictively – The Plattsburgh Town Board Thursday night passed a resolution zoning Crab Island land conservation. Land conservation, one of the most restrictive classifications, limits development to agricultural operations, parks, playgrounds, athletic fields, gold courses, riding academies and game preserves, and accessory building associated with those operations, but excludes dwellings... Before the vote was taken, Councilman Martin Mannix said that it was brought to the town's attention in May by Town Historian Mary Fogarty that the island wasn't zoned. Mannix said that at that time he found out that there were graves on the island, something the Plattsburgh native said he did not know before. The town board immediately acted on the zoning issue, but let it slide somewhat in the early summer when the state indicated to the town that in a short time it would buy the island.

"When the island was purchased by an individual," Mannix said, "the town proceeded with the action begun several months before. In no way was this zoning of Crab Island a reaction to Jakubowski's purchase of the property..."

"That was a bunch of hogwash, typical of a politician," Frank snorts with disgust. "Pure and simple, Roger's plans for development of the island motivated the town's zoning action, and they were determined to thwart any and all development out there. If the zoning restrictions were not personally directed against Roger, why didn't the town make any move to zone the island during the 18-years it was owned by Mr. Troise?"

"It was a bitter pill for Roger to swallow," Frank recalls. "The strictly politically motivated action stuck a craw in my throat too. Government never ceases to amaze me. After 172 years of ignoring the island, the Town of Plattsburgh governmental body suddenly flexed its muscles to allegedly 'protect' the island's history by passing zoning restrictions, which in essence stymied making the history of the island available for public enjoyment. Roger fought back in the courts, but as in most every legal battle between a private citizen and government, the citizen comes out a loser. Angry, but undaunted in his resolve to clean up the island, Roger asked me to revise our business plan to comply with the zoning restrictions. However, before I could put together an acceptable plan, the group of dissidents opposed to any development of the island, started screaming for the government to reclaim control of the island. They were a small but influential group of citizens, and soon captured the attention of state legislators. Shortly after the enactment of the zoning regulations, Roger was notified that New York State intended to seize ownership of the island by 'eminent domain. The notification indicated that the island would be appraised and Roger would be compensated at the assessed value."

The town zoning restrictions had successfully thwarted Jakubowski's original plans for developing Crab Island and, before the plans could be revised to comply with the zoning restrictions, New York State seized ownership of the island through 'eminent domain.'

The following article appeared in the *Plattsburgh Press-Republican* shortly after the state took control of Crab Island under the headline "DEC to Manage Crab Island as Park." The story: Crab Island, which officially became state property through 'eminent domain' last month, is expected to be transferred to the Department of Environmental Conservation to manage and maintain as a public park. Terry Healey, DEC's regional supervisor of natural resources said Wednesday, "That once the agency receives official jurisdiction over the island, a separate unit management plan will be drawn up. Often areas that are adjacent to each other, or are alike, are lumped together under one management plan, but Crab Island is all by itself," Healey continued,, explaining why a separate plan is necessary. "The management plan will center on the island's historic significance. It will certainly consider the island's historic value, mainly the monument and gravesites. That will be the overriding factor. About 50 American and 100 British soldiers who died in the Battle of Plattsburgh were buried in two unmarked trenches on the island on Sept. 11, 1814. A monument to those soldiers was erected there in 1908 and has since fallen into disrepair. Because of the island's historic importance," Healey said, "I do not anticipate the establishment of picnic areas or campsites there but added that it is too early to say specifically what will or will not be considered in the unit management plan. The historic consideration is the prime emphasis. Upkeep of the monument, and restoration of the plaques and surrounding fence will be the agency's main job. Opening the island extensively to the public with the amount of poison ivy there, would pose a problem, but conducting tours is a possibility. Because of the poison ivy, it might be a good idea to just leave the island as it is and make sure it is protected. We'll have to warn people about the poison ivy. No definite plans for the island have yet been discussed. Once the agency is given jurisdiction of Crab Island, a management plan will likely be devised within six months. It's not a big task," Healey stated. He explained that the highlights would include public hearings and meetings with historic groups....

Frank responds to DEC Supervisor Healey's remarks to the media with a derisive laugh. "What a bunch of bull, just another typical display of political hot air from a phony state bureaucrat! The truth is, seventeen or eighteen years have passed since the state seized ownership of the island and the only things that have been accomplished to preserve the island's history, have been done by private citizens. The only thing the state did, was hire me to remove the remnants of the flagpole when it collapsed on the island, and if not for members of our dive club, the monument plaques would not have been recovered. Private citizen, Roger Harwood – not the state - cleared the area around the monument and keeps the area mowed. Private citizens – not the state - restored the flagpole and reset it on the island, and to this day the state has done nothing to locate and preserve the graves of the American and British dead. Fallen trees and poison ivy are the only adornment for their graveyard. My friend Roger Harwood, a retired teacher who lives along the lake, has given a lot of his time and effort to taking care of Crab Island. Roger faithfully loads his mower on a boat, takes it out to the island and mows around the monument. Roger also built a mock up of the monument on Crab, complete with duplications of the plaques and his work is on display in the Clinton County Historical Society building. When the state seized ownership of the island by invoking eminent domain, Jakubowski was furious! He told me that he wanted me to take a bulldozer out to the island and level it. I told him that his anger was justifiable, but I could not do that to the island. I explained to, Roger that he could go back to Atlantic City and peddle hot dogs, but that I live here and have got to face public sentiment. If I leveled the island, I would be run out of town."

Government's re-acquisition of the island to preserve its history after ignoring it for so many years seemed incongruous to Captain Frank. Scratching his head he explained, "The politically motivated seizure of privately owned property seemed a cruel stroke of irony that would have a more profound negative impact on Crab Island than Roger Jakubowski. I knew that under Jakubowski's ownership the island would be spruced up and its historical significance carefully preserved. Under government ownership (as already proven by years of government neglect) the island would deteriorate and its history would be buried beneath poison ivy. Part of Roger's plan called for refurbishing the monument and flagpole, under government ownership that would not happen. Roger had gone so far as to purchase a new 30' x 30' American Flag and wanted it hoisted on the flagpole. He wanted me to raise the flag and, being a former steeplejack and having worked on flagpoles, I told him that I could do it. After telling him that I would raise the flag, I went out to the island, examined the pole and was dismayed at how it had deteriorated. It didn't look safe to climb, so I contacted Herbie Recore, a friend of mine, who owned a small helicopter. Herbie agreed to hoist me seated in a boson chair to the top of the pole. So one morning, Herbie takes off and after we get out over the island, I am lowered in the boson chair, and there I am swinging back and forth about 50 feet under the helicopter, holding a piece of line in one hand. Herbie hovered over the flagpole and did his best to get me in a position where I could thread the line in the top of the pole. I had misjudged the difficulty of the task and being lifted and lowered while swinging back and forth in that confining little seat gave me a whole new perspective of the word 'impaled.' Rotor wash buffeted me about, and I wasn't able to attach the line. After losing this struggle, we returned to Plattsburgh and I commenced searching for another way to attach line to the pole. I couldn't come up with a plan and it began to seem that an uncooperative ghost controlled that flagpole. During the couple of years Roger owned the island, we were unable to raise that beautiful ensign. In later years, the ghost protecting the flagpole apparently abandoned it, and the pole toppled to the ground."

Jakubowski's anger and frustration subsequent to losing ownership of the island were apparent in his interview by a *Plattsburgh Press-Republican* reporter concerning commemorative plaques that had been removed from the monument. Staff Writer Mitch Rosenquist wrote the following article under the title "Jakubowski Has Crab Island Plaques: Crab Island, the center stage of the 1814 Battle of Plattsburgh, has become a battleground again as Roger Jakubowski, who owned the island until the state took it through eminent domain last month, has the monument's plaques and refuses to give them up without a fight. The two plaques, part of the monument built in 1908 to commemorate the 150 American and British soldiers who died in the Battle of Plattsburgh and buried on the island, were retrieved by the Department of Environmental Conservation and given to Jakubowski in 1986 after vandals had removed them. Ivan Vamos, deputy commissioner for the Office of Parks, Recreation and Historic Preservation, said that vandals had thrown one of the plaques into the water and loosened the other, so DEC removed them and gave them to Jakubowski after he purchased the island in 1986. "I don't think he intends to damage them," Vamos said, "he's just letting us know he still has an interest in Crab Island. I don't believe it is a problem."

Asked Monday if he planned to give the plaques to the state, Jakubowski said, "I don't give anything away. In fact, I don't remember giving them Crab Island. Wait until they find out what else I have," Jakubowski said that this is an ongoing battle between him and the state and that he will keep the plaques until the state makes him a reasonable offer. "I'd like to see the governor come and tell the New Jersey governor that someone has some plaques and they want them back," Jakubowski said from his New Jersey office. Jakubowski said that he did not take the plaques since they were his anyway. And as far as he is concerned, they and the island are still his. "Just wait until they find out what else is missing," he said, referring to the gravesites, but not giving any details. "Hey, when you buy a piece of land, you check it out and see what's there. The state is welcome to negotiate with me about the plaques. I will live up to any part of a bargain I agree to. But why should I give them anything?" he asked. "It's very easy to take property with papers when you're not paying for it," he added. Jakubowski, who is currently appealing the state's eminent domain action, said that giving him $5 million still would not satisfy him. "When the state gives me $5 million, this battle still won't be over. Throwing money at it won't solve the problem. Crab Island is one of a kind, and I didn't buy it to have it taken away. How can you price something that's one of a kind? There's a Hope Diamond and then there's a 'hope island.'" Jakubowski outbid the state in 1986 when he offered $190,000. Last month, the state took the property through eminent domain and offered Jakubowski $210,000 in compensation."

A few years after the state took ownership of Crab Island, the flagpole collapsed. Frank was involved in removal of its remains from the island and tells the story of the removal and the dedicated work by a group of volunteers who refurbished the pole and restored it on the island. "When the flag pole collapsed, I was hired by the state to go out and remove the remains from the island. I went out with my crane, barge and equipment. The rusted, broken remains were in terrible condition when we brought it into Plattsburgh. The removal was covered by *Staff Writer Jeff Meyers of the Plattsburgh Press-Republican* who wrote, *"Crab Island Flagpole Rescued-State to Study Repair, Replacement*: The yellow rope, tied at one end to a 30-foot-tall metal pole went taut as a winch whined some hundred yards away. The heavy pole was leaning against the old oak tree that it had fallen against more than a year ago. Suddenly, it wobbled and then crashed forward, making a soft thud as it hit the thick underbrush covering Crab Island. The pole was one of four main pieces of the old metal flagpole erected on the island in 1903 in memory of the sailors who had died during the Battle of Plattsburgh and were buried somewhere on the island. During a severe windstorm in the summer of 1996, the pole had fallen from its anchored position. The four large pieces, as well as several smaller parts, had lain where they fell since then while officials decided what to do with them. Tuesday, workers from the New York State Department of Parks, Recreation and Historic Preservation and a crew from Capt. Frank Pabst's salvaging company spent several hours on the island. They pulled the heavy pieces through the poison-ivy-laced brush to the shoreline, where the flagpole was lifted onto a waiting barge."

"It was an unusual operation, but we got everything set up, and it's gone quite well," Pabst said, as he operated the winch aboard his barge. "It's exciting. We've never done anything like this before. We've had to write the book as we go along."

Larry Gobrecht of the Bureau of Historic Sites said, "The state is going to store the flagpole at Point au Roche State Park, and a metals' conservator will examine it to see if anything can be done to repair and restore the artifact. Obviously, there's a lot of rusted metal and a lot of broken and bent parts. We will determine what can be saved and what needs to be replaced. The flagpole was anchored to the Crab Island soil with four metal pipes driven deep into the ground. Workers kept those anchors in the ground, and they will be used again if the flagpole is returned to the island. Our main goal was to get the flagpole off the island before winter. It is important to get it off the dirt and out of moisture. That would only accelerate its deterioration."

Meyers continued, "Having the flagpole on shore will also help historians analyze the artifact. The metal parts were manufactured in St. Louis, but it's not clear whether the pole was installed from pieces while on the island or placed there intact. After a conservator examines the pole's condition, the state has to come up with a plan for restoring it and money to complete the project. Gobrecht said that there was a very good chance the pole would be returned to its original site...The state is also studying a plan to improve recreational access on Crab Island. In the early 1900s, the federal government had developed a memorial park, including the flagpole and the nearby stone monument, which was erected in 1909. "You can still see the recreational enhancements of this area," Gobrecht said. "This area has a lot of recreational potential. It's too bad that more people do not know the significance of this island."

Frank recalls, "Although looking like it was ready for the scrap yard, the flagpole – in itself – was historic and had a great deal of meaning to those of us truly concerned about the preservation of Crab Island history. I am sure Mr. Gobrecht had good intentions but the truth is, the state didn't want to invest much time or money in Crab Island. If not for the devoted efforts of private citizens, the island would still be without a flagpole."

Roger Harwood and John Rock, friends of Frank, examined the rusted skeletal remains and informed Frank that with work, the pole could be refurbished, strengthened and returned to its place of prominence on the island.

Frank relates, "Roger and John have great love for the lake and are dedicated to the care and preservation of Crab Island. Roger is a retired industrial arts teacher and John is retired from a local utility company where he spent his career as a line mechanic. Both men possess a great deal of expertise in the use of tools and construction, so I didn't doubt the veracity of their claim. They recruited a team of volunteers, and over the course of a few years, the group labored hundreds of hours on the project. When they were through the 100-foot tower of steel looked like new and was stronger than its original version. The challenge then became, how to reset the pole on its pedestal out on Crab Island. The problem seemed to be solved when the Vermont National Guard agreed to raise the flagpole using a helicopter. On a fall day in 2004 with clouds building and rain threatening, the huge National Guard helicopter's rotors churned the air, emitting a 'thump-thump' echo across Plattsburgh Bay, as it hoisted the awkward steel column into the sky and headed for Crab Island. An excited and jubilant restoration crew waited to receive the flagpole on the island, eagerly anticipating being able to tighten the bolts that would secure the pole in place. The helicopter quickly traversed the mile channel and was soon hovering over the small glade that awaited the return of its honored sentry. However, unexpected gusting winds buffeted the pole making it extremely difficult to straighten and align on its pedestal. It seemed to the workers that some unseen force was rebelling against the pole's return. The unsuccessful struggle to erect the pole continued for about an hour. Suddenly, the lines securing the pole to the helicopter gave way and the 100-foot steel tower crashed to the ground. Fortunately, the ground crew managed to scurry out of the way and no physical injuries occurred, although as they gazed upon their now broken labor of love all were momentarily overcome by emotional pain. However, after the clearing of lumps from throats and wiping away sweat and tears, the stalwart group started discussing how they could repair the damage, for this unforeseen setback was not about to prevent them from achieving their goal. The group worked diligently to restore the flagpole - a second-time - and managed to accomplish the task in a few short months. During the restoration they devised a new-plan to erect the huge pole. The equipment and tools necessary to get the job done were brought out to the island by boat, and this time, a block and tackle was erected to lift the pole in place. Members of the flagpole restoration committee, joined by a small group of private citizens truly devoted to the preservation of Crab Island history, gathered in a glade on the southwest end of the island, to witness the hoisting of America's great ensign. It was a proud and happy moment for all as Old Glory rose above treetops and, aided by a breeze, began snapping a salute in tribute to the island that contributed to America's freedom. Anyway - no thanks to the state – Old Glory once again watches over the island and pays tribute to fallen heroes. It gives me a good feeling to see this great symbol of freedom, standing proud among the tallest trees."

Crab Island Flagpole

In June 2004, the retired Captain of the *Juniper* came out of retirement to take command of the *"Weatherwax"* a reproduction of an original Lake Champlain sail ferry, which commenced tours to Crab Island from Plattsburgh. Captain Frank had at last succeeded in realizing part of his dream by proudly introducing passengers to the island he loves and educating them to its history.

Frank still hopes to see Crab Island given the respect and recognition it deserves and relates, "My friend, Assemblyman Chris Ortloff has given me hope that – at long last – the Town of Plattsburgh is moving in the right direction. Chris has publicly proposed that a historical museum be developed on the former Plattsburgh Air Force Base, which will provide visitors tours out to Crab Island. I would envision that Crab Island, with a little bit of marketing, could become a historical destination, not unlike Sturbridge Village over in Vermont. The problem facing this development is that the Clinton County Historical Society has always been stuffy and concerned more with genealogy than with the historic heritage that we have here. I think Chris is beginning to gather support for his proposal and that members of the historical society are getting on board. The ultimate goal, I envision would be to have a museum at the base with a shuttle boat going to Crab Island, trails opened on the island, so that people can walk around it and conclude their visit with a picnic. Secondary to that, a complete museum that would show visitors the important role the lake played in the shaping and development of America; right from the lake's formation after the ice-age, through Champlain's discovery, the French occupation, British occupation, Revolutionary War, War of 1812, and finally, through the development of Plattsburgh Air Force Base."

The Captain's Table

Frank attests, "Throughout the first 25 years of our marriage, Ann and I rarely went out dinner. The reason was my busy schedule and even when there was time, I didn't have any money. When we first married," Frank relates displaying a warm sense of nostalgia, "Ann and I had a wealth of love, but I often didn't have any change in my pockets, let alone dollar bills, so going out to dine in a restaurant was a rare treat. However, I did make it a priority to take Ann to a nice restaurant on each of our wedding anniversaries. Somehow, I got the impression that restaurant owners made bundles of money and most led lives of ease. My having worked one winter season as a bartender at the popular and successful Tijuana Jail Restaurant in Plattsburgh contributed to that belief. The Tijuana Jail did a thriving business and I knew the owners had a fine home on the lake, so I presumed they were rolling in dough. So, I secretly harbored the desire to own and operate a restaurant. Usually, on our wedding anniversary, I'd take Ann to a restaurant located on the corner of Bridge Street and City Hall Place in Plattsburgh. It didn't have the greatest ambiance; however, the food was decent and it's location – just a few blocks from our home – allowed me to enjoy dry martinis without worry about getting home safely. Always curious, friendly and talkative, I got to know the gentleman who held the lease on the restaurant and he told me that he was looking for someone to purchase the lease because he was leaving the area. I made him an offer and obtained the lease for about $10,000. It cost me another $10,000 to refurbish the electric wiring to bring the service up to the required code. After jumping through all the hoops (meeting city zoning requirements) set up by the city and county health department, we established the décor in a theme that would promote the *Juniper*, as well as Lake Champlain, and greeted our first guests at The Captain's Table on New Year's Eve in 1988. It was a proud and happy moment for Ann and me. We offered limousine service door-to-door that evening for all our patrons. Most of the advertising for our grand opening was by word of mouth, but our location at a busy hub in downtown Plattsburgh, was an additional draw. Naturally, our menu focused heavily on seafood and we served fresh lobster. As The Captain's Table carte du jour centered around seafood, we decided that as long as we were ordering large quantities of lobster, shrimp, crab, clams, mussels, fish, etc., having a seafood store in conjunction with the restaurant would allow us to get better prices from the wholesaler. We were fortunate to acquire a location on City Hall Place, just a few doors from The Captain's Table, and named our seafood store, Oceans Harvest. Both business's started off well and I got the bright idea to provide sidewalk service from the restaurant, which was a new concept in Plattsburgh. Sidewalk service required revision of city law and getting permission from the Alcohol Beverage Control Board. It was a hassle, but approval was finally received. The only problem was that the approval came on October 28th, and as you can imagine, there wasn't much call for sidewalk service during the harsh North Country winter. I would attest that The Captain's Table offered the finest food in the area, we developed a good reputation, and every night one could sit at a table located in front of a window and watch drug deals going on across the street. I informed the Mayor and Chief of Police and invited them to come to the Captain's Table, sit in a window seat and see for themselves the criminal activity that was going on. They gave me lip service, but they either didn't have a clue, or didn't care, so there was little enforcement and the neighborhood wasn't to appealing to honest, law-abiding citizens. However, administrations change and with change, I started receiving action. The police started arresting the druggies and today, the area is attractive and considered an upscale neighborhood. Before going into the restaurant business, the only thought I gave to problems that I might encounter were dealing with obnoxious drunks and people complaining about their service. I didn't give much thought to the problems we would encounter in the actual operation of the restaurant. The Captains Table was doing a brisk business and I worked out a deal with a store located just a few doors from the restaurant to sell fresh seafood. One of my favorite memories of the Captains Table restaurant was our New Year's Eve program. I brought in an excellent band for entertainment and we offered the public an all-you-can eat surf and turf dinner, with Champagne, party favors and a free limo ride home, all at a price that other restaurants couldn't compete with. It was a hoot and everyone had a lot of fun. By all appearances, our restaurant was doing a good business, so when Ann, who kept the books, informed me that we were fast losing money and in the red, I couldn't understand it.

At the time, I was operating the *Juniper* three seasons of the year, engaged in lake salvage, doing underwater diving and wasn't paying much attention to the operation of my restaurant. I didn't realize I had a lot of people working for me who apparently thought they were business partners rather than employees. They were taking 'stuff' home and selling 'stuff' out the back door of the restaurant. Also, unknown to me for quite some time, my chef was peddling home grown marihuana out the back door. The way I found out that my chef – who was a graduate of the highly acclaimed Culinary Institute of America, located in Hyde Park and an excellent cook – was into using and selling marihuana was an experience I would prefer to forget. One afternoon, I was in the *Captains Table* and saw a pan of freshly baked brownies cooling on the counter. I helped myself to a brownie and it was delicious, so I ate a couple more. Shortly after consuming the brownies, I started feeling woozy and decided to lie down for a bit to shake off whatever was ailing me. We kept a cot in the basement office, so I went down to the basement and stretched out on the cot. As I was lying there, I started hallucinating and thought that someone was in the room and they were trying to stab me with a large knife. I had experienced hangovers resulting from the liberal consumption of my favorite beverages before, but this dizziness accompanied by a feeling of paranoia, was worse than any previous hangover, and as I had not had an alcoholic drink that day, I was at a loss as to what was ailing me. I considered calling Ann and asking her to take me to the hospital; however, before I did, my chef appeared and asked me if I had gotten into 'his' brownies. I told him that, in fact, I had and they were delicious, but I was concerned what he had put in them because they might be responsible for my feeling so weird. He told me that the brownies were his own 'special' recipe and they contained a liberal amount of marihuana. That was my first and only experience with marihuana and it left me wondering why anyone would want to smoke or ingest that crap. Needless to say, I was angry with my chef, but his father was a good friend of mine and I had known the son from the time he was a little kid. He frequently was a source of consternation and created problems, but I loved him and couldn't get too angry with him. Despite a brisk business The Captains Table continued losing money and I couldn't figure out a way of curing the problem. Our debts mounted and I was forced to declare bankruptcy in 1989. I closed the restaurant, seafood store, and we lost two houses that I had purchased as investment property, but I managed to keep the *Juniper*.

Many of our financial problems stemmed from the fires that we had at our warehouse on the waterfront. I lost $250,000 as a result of the first fire and we were still reeling when the second one happened. I loved the restaurant business, but as a party animal, I was one of my own best customers and I didn't pay enough attention to the cause of our losing money. After going through bankruptcy, I told Ann that if I ever got the inclination to open another restaurant, or a trucking company, she should hire a huge oriental and have him perform acupuncture on my brain."

Raising the Confiance Anchor

The salvage business required a lot of equipment and, over time, Frank accumulated barges, an old tugboat and cranes; however, the *Juniper* was the mainstay of the business.

Frank relates, "We 'acquired' the tug *Eighth Sea* from the Saint Lawrence Seaway Authority and my buddy, Bill, put up the dough for this purchase. I suggested we bid $25,000.99 for the tug as a competing bid against a bid of $25,000 offered by McLain Towing, located in Hamilton, Ontario. After we took possession of the tug, McLain offered Bill $35,000 for it. Bill didn't sell it and he still has the tug and it is now berthed down in the Port of Albany. We also had a 50foot barge that held one of my cranes. The tug was an old army tug. We sailed it from Massena to Plattsburgh, up the Saint Lawrence to Three Rivers, and then down the Chambley Canal to Lake Champlain; it was a great ride. The tug served us well on Lake Champlain and it was used in a number of salvage jobs. I had sonar on the tug and one day in 1996, while in Cumberland Bay, the sonar echoed on a large object on the bottom of the lake. The location was noted on our GPS and after returning to the dock, we provided the location of the object to Bill Van Stockum, a diving friend. We knew the sonar hit was something of significance because another sonar hit on an area about 200 yards from the first hit, indicated a 60' x 200' field of debris. After discussing this find, we decided that the debris was from the *Confiance,* and represented items thrown overboard while clearing its deck for action.

The Van Stockum's went out to search the area, and found a large object, but the visibility was so poor, they couldn't tell what it was. Ken Van Stockum went out again with John Lambrinos and they found that it was a huge anchor."

The *Plattsburgh Press-Republican* continues the story in an article written by Staff Writer Jeff Meyers, which appeared in the January 8, 2001 edition, under the caption *Anchor Man Relives Underwater Discovery.* "Visibility is poor 60feet below the surface of Lake Champlain. Objects on the lake bottom – half buried in the muck that has lain there for thousands of years – appear surreal, distorted by the depths. It was late August when John Lambrinos slowly made his way along the murky bottom of Cumberland Bay. A day earlier, fellow diver Kenneth Van Stockum had spotted a large object in the area, and the two had returned to see if they could find it again.

"After 50 minutes of diving, I had not seen anything on the bottom," Lambrinos said from his Plattsburgh restaurant, Gus's Red Hots. "I was getting ready to end my dive and surface, when I saw something in the distance protruding up from the bottom." Lambrinos swam over to the object and clearly saw a wooden crosspiece with a metal ring attached. The shaft of what was obviously a large anchor disappeared underneath the mud. "I knew right away it was the largest anchor I'd ever seen," Lambrinos said. "At the time, I didn't think it was going to be such a historic moment."

Lambrinos tied a buoy to the relic and released the marker to the surface, forever securing a place in history.

The anchor, it turns out, came from the British flagship *Confiance,* the lead vessel, in the fleet that attacked a much smaller American force during the Sept. 11, 1814 battle, which, subsequently would be enshrined in history as the Battle of Plattsburgh. In fact, history experts believe one of the key reasons the British lost the battle was that the *Confiance* lost an anchor to American cannon fire early in the contest, causing the ship to lose its maneuverability. A few years before he and the Van Stockums came across the *Confiance* anchor, Lambrinos found another anchor in Cumberland Bay that also probably came from the Battle of Plattsburgh. It's about half the size of the anchor on display at City Hall. Lambrinos has put it on display in his back yard, surrounded by cannonballs he has also fished from the lake. But he says that it and other artifacts from the lake should be on display for the public to see and hopes that a future Battle of Plattsburgh museum will open to provide a viewing area. "I can definitely contribute a lot of artifacts," he said. When the buoy Lambrinos used floated to the surface, he signaled for William Van Stockum, Kenneth's father, who was waiting for the two divers aboard his boat. The senior Van Stockum tied up to the buoy, and the three men returned to the anchor for another glimpse. They obtained the services of Captain Frank Pabst and returned the next day to retrieve their find. But in the shuffle of excitement and media coverage, Lambrinos' role in the find became lost, and the unassuming restaurant owner never came forward to stake his claim in the historic moment.

"It was a team effort to find it, buoy it and recover it," he said recently. "It wasn't just a one-man or two-man operation."

Lambrinos came to the North Country in 1974. His wife's father was a previous owner of Gus' Red Hots. Lambrinos first tried diving in the late 1970s, while vacationing in the Caribbean. The diving bug caught him, and he found himself entering Lake Champlain more and more often. "There's not really much to see in the lake other than looking for artifacts and old relics," he said. "It's exciting when you think you're in an area and finding cannonballs that haven't been seen by people in more than 200 years." He has a lot of his finds on display at the restaurant, where he has a cabinet full of old glass bottles dating back as far as the 1700s. He also has a painting in his dining area depicting the naval fight during the Battle of Plattsburgh. The painting was done by an employee and given to Lambrinos…"

As Lambrinos indicated, raising the 14-by-13 foot anchor, weighing approximately 3000 pounds, was trusted to Captain Frank Pabst, who was pleased and proud to take part in raising the venerable piece of American history.

"Although it (the anchor) was found in 1996," Frank relates, "we didn't haul it up until 1998. The finding was kept sort of quiet until a determination could be made that the anchor was actually from the *Confiance*. When it was identified, the politicians wrangled as to who was going to pay to salvage it and where the famous anchor would be kept. At the same time, the City of Plattsburgh was trying to seize my leased little cove on the lake and force me out of business. My relationship with the city administration was tenuous to say the least. Some in the administration praised me publicly, but privately they considered me a pariah. Nevertheless, when it came to salvaging large objects from the lake, I was about the only act in town. Raising the *Confiance* anchor was one of the most exciting moments in my life. As the huge, flanged piece of steel, resembling a gigantic fishhook rose above the surface of the lake, and knowing the role it played in the shaping of America, made me awestruck. And being able to readily see the indentation on the fluke that was caused by a cannonball, made it even more awesome. Of course, numerous cameras were on hand to record the moment. After raising the anchor, we brought it into our cove, and then the decision was made to transport it down to the Lake Champlain Maritime Museum in Basin Harbor, Vermont. We delivered it to the museum for restoration, and I believed after it was restored, it would remain in the museum. It was held on display at the Maritime Museum for a time, but then members of the Plattsburgh City Council started raising a ruckus because they believed the famous anchor belonged in Plattsburgh. A tug of war ensued between politicians as to where the anchor should be put on 'permanent' display, and eventually the City of Plattsburgh won."

Raising Confiance Anchor

Anchor on Surface

Confiance Anchor at Dock

Most Famous Anchor

Confiance Anchor on Shore part 1

Confiance Anchor on Shore Part 2

The historic anchor from the British Warship Confiance is recovered from the depths of Cumberland Bay. (2000)

Confiance Anchor on Shore Part 3

This report was written by Staff Writer Joe LoTemplio and published in the *Plattsburgh Press-Republican* on August 5, 2000, under the caption *Prized Anchor Set for Display, but City May Face Jurisdictional Dispute* sums up the contest. "City councilors agreed to pay for the transportation and display of a historic battleship anchor as long as they can keep it forever. But the man who dragged the anchor out of Lake Champlain says the city should not be making such decisions.

'That anchor does not belong to the city, and they have no business voting on it,' said Frank Pabst, a marine-salvage operator who hauled the 3000-pound anchor from the British warship *Confiance* out of the lake.

At Thursday night's meeting, councilors agreed to spend $4,200 to transport, handle and display the 14-by-13 foot anchor that fell to the lake floor during the Battle of Plattsburgh in 1814. The anchor was first discovered in 1996 but was not retrieved from the water until 1998. It has since been housed at the Lake Champlain Maritime Museum in Burlington, Vt., where it has been restored and prepared for open-air display. The anchor is now ready for transport and is due to arrive at City Hall on Aug. 24. The plan is to display the anchor in the rotunda of City Hall in front of the Common Council chambers.

City Engineer George Miller said that 'the bottom of the anchor will be placed near the entrance to the rotunda and the crossbar will be near the council chamber doors. It will be set on an angle on a steel platform and roped off to the public. The anchor is the property of New York State, which was looking for a temporary – three to five years – site to house it - until it could be placed at the historical museum planned for the former Plattsburgh Air Force Base property.'

But councilors Terry Gordon and Jack Stewart said the anchor should be kept at City Hall permanently. 'If we are going to pay $4,200 to have it brought over here, I don't want someone coming in a month from now and taking it,' Gordon said. Gordon amended the resolution to pay for the transport of the anchor to say that it will be kept on "permanent display" in City Hall.

Stewart, a local history expert, said, 'Removing the anchor from City Hall would be tantamount to sacrilege. The Battle of Plattsburgh was fought here, not out at the Air Force Base,' Stewart boomed. 'This is the best home they (the state) could ever give it.'

Stewart also said that such a historical attraction downtown would be important for businesses, which want to attract tourist dollars.

However Pabst, who said he spent $7,000 of his own money to retrieve the anchor and bring it to Burlington, said it was the discovery of the anchor that sparked talk of a historical museum at the base in the first place. 'Nobody ever bothers to remember that,' he said. 'It belongs permanently at a museum in a National Parks site because that's where the real tourist attractions are.'

Stewart said the proposed national park at the base ' will never happen. That's just pie in the sky,' he said. Stewart also said that having the anchor in City Hall would work in conjunction with the Macdonough Monument – located across the street as a tourist site.

Assemblyman Chris Ortloff, who is spearheading the effort to create a museum at the base, said there is no point in arguing over a display site at this point because City Hall is the only place it can really be kept. He disputed Stewart's assertion that the park at the base will never materialize. 'I would hope that he would have a bigger vision for the city,' Ortloff said. 'The governor (George Pataki) asked me about it last night, and anytime you have a governor that interested in something, I think it's shortsighted to say that it's not going to happen.'

While the city may have voted to keep the anchor permanently, it is not a binding vote, according to one state official. Phil Lord of the State Museum in Albany, who said, 'the anchor belongs to the people of the state and no local government body can vote to keep it permanently.' He also said that, 'while museums may be the preferred site for such an item because they are more accessible to school groups, the state's main concern is that the artifact is secure.' Lord said, 'City Hall would be a suitable place to display the anchor until a museum is developed, at which time a decision could be made. If there ever was a real dispute, I suppose we'd try to develop some sort of agreement,' Lord said.

Along with Stewart and Gordon, Councilors Roland Lockwood and Harold "Rebel" Hicks voted in favor of keeping the anchor permanently at City Hall. Councilor Joseph Lombardoni voted against it because he felt the city might not have the authority to do so. Councilor Christine Rotella and Mayor Daniel Stewart were not at the meeting.

Pabst said the vote was out of line. 'Now I know who I can send my $7,000 bill to,' he said."

As of this writing, the historic *Confiance* anchor is on display inside Plattsburgh City Hall and Frank Pabst is yet to be paid for causing the anchor to be there.

Epilogue

Although now in his 70s, the Captain of *The Juniper* is as spirited and ebullient as ever, and possesses the stamina of many men half his age. Oh sure, the rocking, side-to-side gait, inherent to men of the sea has slowed somewhat, but the Captain still sports a thick mane of white hair, his quick wit has not diminished, and he continues to uniquely respond to people in a short, quaint, salty-tongued, proverbial fashion. Retirement is out of the question for the ever-ambitious Captain and eternal entrepreneur. No work has ever been, nor will ever be below his dignity, and despite all of the extraordinary accomplishments in his life, that set him apart and above most ordinary men, he considers himself an ordinary man and is more comfortable with ordinary men. Frank remains active in promoting the historical aspects of Lake Champlain and in 2001, again teamed with his old friend Billy Reid to promote the anniversary of the *Battle of Valcour,* and would be cited by another living legend of the North Country, Gordon "Gordie" Little, for his work in preserving Lake Champlain history.

In his "Small Talk" column, published January 28, 2001 in the *Plattsburgh Press-Republican,* Gordie spoke of his relationship with Frank Pabst, in an article titled: *Healthy Interest in History is Heart- warming.* He wrote: "Finally. People all over the area seem to be gaining interest in local history. I'm very pleased. Young people are interviewing their grandparents for school projects. Sons and daughters are videotaping their parents' lives' stories. Municipalities are making big deals out of their histories. Old photographs, paintings, maps, diaries and journals are being discovered and made public. People are scouring their attics for artifacts. This newspaper is printing frequent articles with their focus on local history. Public-access cable channels are running more and more historical subject matter. The television and radio stations often do features on area history. It all counts. Hopefully, we'll have that proposed interpretive center at the Old Stone Barracks on the former Plattsburgh Air Force Base. Hopefully, someone will come up with the money to pay for that Battle of Plattsburgh mural we heard so much about more than a year ago. I am confident that the annual commemoration of that famous naval battle will grow in scope and popularity each year as we work toward the bicentennial in 2014. It surely makes getting up in the morning more exciting for me. There is always something new to add to the history pot. Plattsburgh City Clerk Keith Herkalo is relentless in ferreting out tidbits, which he often shares with me then with the rest of the world. I'm honored. We have a couple pieces of the *Royal Savage* here, and maybe we can negotiate to get the rest of remains of that famous ship back here where it belongs. Others are doing the same in their own special ways. More and more area citizens are becoming re-enactors and are compiling their own genealogy. We hear that heritage tourism is growing by leaps and bounds. I hate to say I told you so, but I told you so! Captain Frank Pabst and I did countless radio interviews decades ago to try and generate interest in preserving things taken from Lake Champlain. We were constantly frustrated in our efforts and often lamented that our history pitch was falling on deaf ears. I'm thrilled to report that those efforts, added to many others, are really starting to bear fruit…"

In the August 1, 2001 edition of the *Plattsburgh Press-Republican*, Staff Writer Jeff Meyers wrote under the caption: *Aiming for Big Doings – Battle of Valcour Fete Set.* "Canon fire along the shores of Lake Champlain will signal the region's appreciation for one of the most significant naval battles of the Revolutionary War. Local history buffs have organized a celebration of Benedict Arnold and the Battle of Valcour Island, a conflict in which a fledgling American fleet held off a vastly superior British Navy long enough to turn the war in America's favor…

'It's a commemorative celebration of the gallantry and patriotism of our forefathers,' said Battle of Valcour Committee Chairman Frank Pabst. 'Against overwhelming odds, they (the American fleet) stopped and defended the colors of this country. This is a celebration to pay our respects to those men.'

On Oct. 11, 1776, the American fleet of about a dozen ships lay anchored in the lake between Valcour Island and the New York shore as the invading British fleet passed the island off Valcour's eastern shore en route to Albany in an effort to capture the Lake Champlain corridor. The British ships were about two miles south of Valcour when they first spotted the American boats. With a strong southerly wind, the enemy had a difficult time turning around to engage the Americans. Although the invading fleet eventually defeated the Americans, Arnold's efforts prevented the British from reaching Ticonderoga that year. That forced them to turn back to Canada for the winter, giving the Americans time to prepare for a convincing win at Saratoga in 1777. Russell Bellico, noted author of a history of Lake Champlain, will be on hand during the anniversary celebration to share stories and a slide show about the significance of the Battle of Valcour and the Lake Champlain Corridor. Hudson Haaglund, whose father raised the American vessels Philadelphia and Royal Savage from near Valcour Island in the 1930s, will discuss his father's efforts in saving a piece of the lake's history. Local diver Ed Scollon will share his experiences in finding the American cannon that was recently raised from the battle site...Local storyteller and singer Stan Ransom will be on hand to entertain.

'I didn't want the carnival atmosphere that you'll find at the Battle of Plattsburgh celebration,' Pabst said. "We'll be focusing more on the historical perspective of this battle and the men's valiant efforts.'"

Tributes to the Captain

Frank Pabst is the sort of storied enigmatic individual who inspires a broad range of emotions in people. Those individuals who spent time with him, dove beneath the surface of the water with him, tipped beers with him and came to know and appreciate his quick wit and pleasant, humorous personality, love him. Frank's detractors number far fewer than his friends and many of these detractors have formed their opinion based on the physical appearance of his lakeside business operation and they refused to get to know Frank. Whether friend or foe, almost everyone in the North Country would agree that the salty transplant to the North Country from New York City, had become a virtual living legend of Lake Champlain.

In an exchange of emails, Gordie Little would attest to that fact. He would add, "Frank certainly is a colorful personality. He is a good friend and his wife Annie is a very special lady. Frank taught me how to dive by strapping on a tank and telling me to jump in the lake. On a dive in Lake Champlain, I suddenly found it was becoming difficult to breathe, thought I was running out of air, and that I was going to die. I grabbed Frank who was nearby and, seeing the sheer panic in my eyes, he simply reached over my shoulder and opened the valve of my auxiliary air. Frank and I have had some shiny and some tarnished moments over the past four decades or so. Ask him about the Christmas party we held once on the bottom of the YMCA pool. There are photos of the event somewhere. We took a trip or two to the Country and Western bars in Montreal that probably set some records. The trips to and from Montreal, over icy, winter roads, in his old Cadillac were memorable, to say the least. Ask Frank about his taking me to an area near where you will now find the entrance to the

Ausable Chasm Campground to see the skeletal remains to a famous Lake Champlain Steamboat. I was with Frank when the cannon were raised off Cliff Haven. It was captured for posterity on reel-to-reel audiotape. I followed and reported on the controversy over ownership of the cannon for many years. I interviewed Frank numerous times on both radio and television. Frank's tremendous generosity in giving the less advantaged guys and gals jobs on and off the boat is legendary. His knowledge and passion for local lake region history made every *Juniper* ride an enjoyable experience. The Wreck Raiders defined scuba diving in this area and those stories alone are enough to fill one or two volumes."

The Reverend John Sorensen former Pastor of Trinity Church in Plattsburgh, present Pastor of Saint John's Church in Glen Mills, Pennsylvannia submits: "Bob Goetz, Press Republican Sports Editor and a former parishioner of mine in Plattsburgh, sent along to me your request for stories about Frank Pabst. Frank was a parishioner of mine at Trinity Church in Plattsburgh, and I got to know him well in that capacity. We became even better acquainted when we founded the Sea Scouts ship about 2004, his days helping commission and operate the flat-bottomed sailing ferry, with regular trips to Crab Island and sometimes Valcour; for the Transportation Museum from about 2004-2006; his being bought out of his lease with the rail yard by the city so they could build a dock; the ill fated year of the *Spirit of Plattsburgh* and the shoddy service that made the *Juniper* replacement a failure (they should have hired Frank to run it); the lease of the *Juniper* to a doctor who backed out and the boat's being cut up for scrap. Frank then became Captain of our Soup Kitchen at the church on land and he demonstrated that he has a great heart for the poor in downtown. Frank is a remarkable and fine man."

Jessica Cupoli of Syracuse New York, submits: "I have been fortunate enough to be friends with Ann and Frank for 20 wonderful years. In 1986, I was lucky enough to be invited by my Agent, Chandler Atwater, to a summer Underwriter Appreciation Day that was celebrated on the *Juniper*. Although I had traveled to Plattsburgh several times before this, I had only attended family members' weddings at the base Officers Club. Suffice it to say, Captain Frank opened my eyes to a whole different Plattsburgh – in fact – to a whole different world! I never had met ANY one like him, so smart, so passionate about the Lake, the history of Plattsburgh, and well, let's face it – just so unique and cool! I had business dealings in the North Country and, for many years after that, I managed to get back every summer to catch a ride with Frank. I was even able to entertain some clients with a boat ride, and the result was ALWAYS the same. Great food, great ride, great people, and oh, what a lake! (Frank will tell you, I am a Polar Bear) I learned so much about the North Country from him, Plattsburgh just doesn't seem the same to me without the *Juniper*. I miss it terribly, and also so many other businesses that have gone the way of "progress" and gentrification – the Tijuana Jail was one. One thing that NEVER changes is Frank, and I will always be eternally grateful for that!"

The former Captain of, *The Juniper*, is now Captain of *The Weatherwax*, a restored, sail ferryboat that once carted humans, animals and goods across Lake Champlain in the vicinity of the present day Crown Point Bridge, circa 1800 and which today carries passengers between the former Plattsburgh Air Force Base and Crab and Valcour Islands. Although smaller, slower (a small outboard engine supplements the sail) and not as seaworthy as the *Juniper*, passengers are awed by the scenic beauty of the lake and a memorable history lesson from a man who loves the lake with all his heart.

An editorial in the April 18, 2003 edition of the *Plattsburgh Press-Republican* titled, *Frank Pabst: a Worthy Legacy* provides an excellent analogy as to some of the reasons – but only some – as to how a poorly educated product of New York City achieved the distinction of becoming a living legend of Lake Champlain. The editorial began by noting a mention in the paper's "The Week in Sports," which ran in Monday's edition, under the section "40 years ago (in 1963) and stated: "The Lake Champlain Underwater Research club, led by Frank Pabst and Roy Holt, push for a museum at 75 Miller St. to commemorate naval battles."

"That museum never came to pass. Like many ventures in which Pabst was to align himself over the next four decades, its potential was never realized. Frank Pabst has been many things to many people over the years, but one thing he surely was – and for which he has always been under- appreciated – was a visionary. Pabst was one of the first around here to foresee the value of Lake Champlain as a depository of history. And not just history on the fringes of general interest. He knew Lake Champlain played a pivotal role in the birth and adolescence of our nation. Not only that, he knew that role was a highly salable commodity that had the potential to bring in visitors from all over the country, if not the world. So, 40 years ago, his diving team had collected an impressive sample of relics from the bottom of the lake that told stories of landmark battles in the Revolutionary War and the War of 1812. At the time, unfortunately, only he and his fellow divers realized how important these relics were. Pabst tried to interest the community and the state in establishing the Miller Street museum, near his house, so the public could view the artifacts, learn the history and try to exploit this fecund resource. His entreaties fell on deaf ears, as his entreaties often did. The community showed no interest in the history he was laying at its feet, and the state, rather than applauding his resourcefulness, acted somewhat antagonistically toward his efforts. Funding never materialized. All the relics that had been raised – cannonballs, parts of ships of battle and many other items that bore witness to great events – wound up in the possession of divers. Many are still around, awaiting delivery to a naval museum, if it's ever established. Local interest in such a project is now high. It will probably happen. At that point, we're guessing Frank Pabst's name will be a footnote, at best. As usual, his contributions will be overlooked. When he was unceremoniously bought out of his shoreline enterprises two years ago, he conceded some bitterness over the fact that he was never given his due as a dispenser of local history. When he ran his tour boat, he alone was keeping the lake's legacy in the forefront of people's awareness. It was he who nourished the notion that we live in a cradle of American history. He deserves credit for at least that."

Author comment: A large monument on the western shore of Lake Champlain, at the point where the Saranac River empties into the lake, in the City of Plattsburgh, pays tribute to Samuel de Champlain, the lake's namesake. Another large monument located across from Plattsburgh City Hall, pays tribute to Commodore Thomas Macdonough, who led the American naval force that defeated the British in 1814. It would seem appropriate to erect a 'small' monument, or perhaps a plaque on a polished stone, in the City's newly created park at lakeside, in honor of *Frank Pabst, The Captain of The Juniper* who contributed so much to Lake Champlain and the City of Plattsburgh. However, that is but a dream that will most certainly never be fulfilled in my lifetime, because Captain Pabst had, and continues to have a knack for ruffling the feathers of politicians when he disagrees with them.

Such recognition is of no consequence or importance to Captain Frank Pabst, who attests, "My family, my many friends and Lake Champlain have provided me so much pleasure, so much joy, so much prosperity, so much love, how could I ask for more?"